Real Life Financial Planning for Young Lawyers

A Young Lawyer's Guide to Building
the Financial House of Their Dreams

Thomas A. Haunty, CFP®, RHU, REBC, ChFC
Todd D. Bramson, CFP®, ChFC, CLU

BOOK IDEA SUBMISSIONS

If you are a C-Level executive or senior lawyer interested in submitting a book idea or manuscript to the Aspatore editorial board, please email authors@aspatore.com. Aspatore is especially looking for highly specific book ideas that would have a direct financial impact on behalf of a reader. Completed books can range from 20 to 2,000 pages – the topic and "need to read" aspect of the material are most important, not the length. Include your book idea, biography, and any additional pertinent information.

ARTICLE SUBMISSIONS

If you are a C-Level executive or senior lawyer interested in submitting an article idea (or content from an article previously written but never formally published), please email authors@aspatore.com. Aspatore is especially looking for highly specific articles that would be a part of our Executive Reports series. Completed reports can range from 2 to 20 pages and are distributed as coil-bound reports to bookstores nationwide. Include your article idea, biography, and any additional information.

GIVE A VIDEO LEADERSHIP SEMINAR

If you are interested in giving a Video Leadership Seminar, please email the ReedLogic Speaker Board at speakers@reedlogic.com (a partner of Aspatore Books). If selected, ReedLogic would work with you to identify the topic and create interview questions. You would then have someone videotape you answering the questions. ReedLogic producers then cut the video and turn it into a segment that is like a seminar teaching the viewer on your area of expertise. The final product is burned onto DVD and distributed to bookstores nationwide.

Published by Aspatore Inc.

For corrections, company/title updates, comments, or any other inquiries, please e-mail store@aspatore.com.

First Printing, 2006
10 9 8 7 6 5 4 3 2 1

Copyright © 2006 by Todd D. Bramson. All rights reserved. Printed in the United States of America. No part of this publication may be reproduced or distributed in any form or by any means, or stored in a database or retrieval system, except as permitted under Sections 107 or 108 of the U.S. Copyright Act, without prior written permission of the publisher. This book is printed on acid-free paper.

ISBN 1-59622-541-6
Library of Congress Control Number: 2006928107

Managing Editor, Laura Kearns, Edited by Eddie Fournier

Material in this book is for educational purposes only. This book is sold with the understanding that neither any of the authors nor the publisher is engaged in rendering legal, accounting, investment, or any other professional service. Neither the publisher nor the authors assume any liability for any errors or omissions, or for how this book or its contents are used or interpreted, or for any consequences resulting directly or indirectly from the use of this book. For legal advice or any other, please consult your personal lawyer or the appropriate professional.

The views expressed by the individuals in this book (or the individuals on the cover) do not necessarily reflect the views shared by the companies they are employed by (or the companies mentioned in this book). The employment status and affiliations of authors with the companies referenced are subject to change.

Aspatore Books is the largest and most exclusive publisher of C-Level executives (CEO, CFO, CTO, CMO, Partner) from the world's most respected companies and law firms. Aspatore annually publishes a select group of C-Level executives from the Global 1,000, top 250 law firms (Partners and Chairs), and other leading companies of all sizes. C-Level Business Intelligence™, as conceptualized and developed by Aspatore Books, provides professionals of all levels with proven business intelligence from industry insiders—direct and unfiltered insight from those who know it best—as opposed to third-party accounts offered by unknown authors and analysts. Aspatore Books is committed to publishing an innovative line of business and legal books, those which lay forth principles and offer insights that when employed, can have a direct financial impact on the reader's business objectives, whatever they may be. In essence, Aspatore publishes critical tools – need-to-read as opposed to nice-to-read books – for all business professionals.

Dedications

This book is dedicated to my wife, Mary Beth. Her constant faith, support, and encouragement continually propel me to grow in Christian faith, in character, and in my financial planning service to others.

Thomas A. Haunty, July 2006

This book is dedicated to my immediate family. Without the love, support, and guidance of all of these people, I wouldn't have learned the most important lesson of life: "When all is said and done, it is the quality and depth of relationships and experiences that are the essence of life…not the accumulation of material possessions."

Todd D. Bramson, July, 2006

Thank You

I owe a special thank you to my clients who over the years have taught me how to make financial planning concepts work practically in their lives.

I also must thank everyone who supports me at North Star Resource Group—our commitments to faith, integrity, growth, and service have been the key ingredients in a culture that has bred my success. Specifically, my practice manager Joni Lownik, Phil Richards, Scott Richards, Dave Vasos, Nick Stevens, Paul Mershon, Diane Yohn, and my partners in the Madison office, Chuck, Brian, Doug, and Todd.

Kelley Ables at the American Bar Endowment (ABE) is owed a special thanks for her trust in me to speak to the many lawyers the ABE serves.

Finally, thanks to *The ABA Journal*—specifically Steve Keeva and Jenny Davis—who readily give me the opportunity to advocate for improving the finances of attorneys.

Thomas A. Haunty, July, 2006

I extend a special thank you to…

…my clients who have trusted me with their financial decisions.

…my staff, partners, and business associates who make work a pleasure.

…Leslie Millikan for listening and offering insight and constructive ideas as my business "coach."

…all of those special people who I have learned from, especially Dick and Kathy Anderson, Ed Deutschlander, John Gadow, Joel Huth, Dick Koob, Bob Logas, Paul Mershon, Phil Richards, Scott Richards, Art Sanger, Herb Schmiedel, Mark Schweiger, Dave Smrecek, Nick Stevens, Dave Vasos, Diane Yohn, Pete and Jody Witte, and Andy, Brad, Dan, Jeff, Pete, and Scott.

Lastly, a special thank you to Mishelle Shepard who kept encouraging and helping me throughout the process of writing this book. This would still be handwritten ideas on a yellow scratch pad if it wasn't for you.

Todd D. Bramson, July 2006

Real Life Financial Planning
for Young Lawyers

CONTENTS

1

Wealth Construction Barriers Lawyers Face

Lawyers spend so much of their time protecting, allocating, litigating over, and negotiating with other people's money, yet many of those same lawyers treat their own finances with a lack of care bordering on negligence.

Cumulatively, we have spent almost fifty years working directly with individuals, answering their questions, and working on their financial plans. In those client meetings, we have met and worked with numerous attorneys and found that this professional group knows a lot about personal finance, yet does not put into practice what they know. The proverbial saying that "the cobbler's kids have holes in their shoes" applies to lawyers. As we were asked by more and more attorneys to help them "do what we did for their clients," it became clear to us that there was a large gap between having knowledge and having the wisdom to apply that knowledge to themselves.

How can a professional group with so much education and intelligence not be achieving the financial success they deserve?

Why don't lawyers attend to their own "financial house" with the same vigor they bring to representing their clients?

What is preventing lawyers from reaching their future financial dreams and goals?

Here is some of the mounting evidence we have collected on the major construction barriers lawyers face today that prevent them from building real wealth.

Lack of Time

Lawyers today are pressed and stressed for time more than ever. Increasing competition between firms and the pressure to hit required billable hours come at the expense of less time to tend to personal needs and even less energy to spend learning about personal financial matters. "Do more, do it faster, and deliver it for less" seems to be a constant mantra at firms. This keeps lawyers so busy working in their law practice that they are too often prevented from properly managing the money their practice creates.

Although capable of quickly learning a tremendous amount of new material from case to case, this skill set lawyers possess does not readily translate into wise financial management. Many lawyers just do not do the homework they should because of a false sense of security that they are already familiar with financial terms and concepts. They often are forced into making more impulsive rather than informed financial decisions. With tax, insurance, and investment options continually multiplying, presenting even more choices, the odds of making financial mistakes are getting increasingly higher.

Procrastination

The temptation to put off financial planning is strong among lawyers who can make many compelling arguments for not starting to develop their plans. Often, they delay implementing important savings and investment strategies early in their careers as they obsess over paying back student loans and believe they must "invest" instead in establishing their new career lifestyles (i.e., clothes, cars, country club memberships, etc.). Then family responsibilities arise and mortgage payments on the new home become the urgent excuses to avoid establishing important wealth-building habits. From there, they continue to pardon themselves from planning until they become partner or win the large contingency case, which is the time they feel they will finally have the income to plan. Then "the big case" never comes, or the money is needed for unforeseen expenses, or that partner-level income does not seem to cover as much as they thought. Most of the time, they focus on the needs of their clients, often to the detriment of themselves, resulting in having to face large expenses like children's college tuition without the needed capital. So they go further into debt to pay for it, delaying any hope of real retirement.

What procrastination steals from lawyers is one of their important assets: the time to let money invested compound into wealth. It also robs them of critical learning and the ingraining of key financial habits that can assure the proper management of the larger partner income and large contingency cases that may come later on. Many attorneys mismanage windfalls of cash all because they never spent the time to learn how to handle that amount of wealth.

Lack of Delegation

Lawyers are trained to take charge and be on top of what's going on for their clients' needs, so they often don't feel comfortable confiding in an advisor about something they think they should already know. Asking for help can seem akin to admitting a professional shortcoming. Also, they fear looking bad publicly for any financial missteps, since lawyers are supposed to be "smart." After all, they are the source of solutions for other people's problems, which are often very complex, so why can't they handle all of their own financial planning?

Do-it-yourself financial planning, though, is fraught with the same problems lawyers can encounter when representing themselves in legal matters. You lose the objectivity needed to consider all the options and issues that can impact your financial decisions.

Despite being highly intelligent critical thinkers on client casework, lawyers also fall into a seductive overconfidence that causes them to overestimate their abilities in handling their personal finances. Familiarity with many aspects of financial planning does not automatically breed the proper implementation of those concepts. Even if you are a "master of the minutia"—understanding all the details and assumptions of an investment deal—it doesn't mean you can control whether it will make money or whether it fits into your overall planning.

In fact, some of the very skills that may help you thrive as a successful lawyer can often keep you from following sound professional financial advice. Skepticism, for example, that the basics of financial planning are too simple, or that earning high investment returns is only done through very complex processes, results in lawyers skipping the foundational basics that build solid long-term wealth. Another example is that some lawyers have developed a low opinion and mistrust of insurance companies, which can make them ignore owning insurance policies which can be valuable risk management tools.

The most successful attorneys we have seen—the senior partners—see themselves first and foremost as entrepreneurs who just happen to be in the business of giving legal advice. They do not "do it all themselves" but succeed more by relying on and managing a team of advisors who cut through the complexity of their lives to free them up so they can focus more time on what their goals and gifts are. A trusted financial advisor, a certified public accountant, and their own attorney form that financial team acting like personal financial "trainers" who continually assist them in getting financially stronger.

Deficit Spending

You cannot build wealth if you keep spending more than you make. Wealth building has more to do with how much you are able to keep, not how much you earn.

Your income now may be below what you are capable of earning, but you cannot always assume you will earn more money "someday." For many lawyers, that future income is highly erratic from year to year and, even in the high-income years, it may not be enough to bail out badly ingrained spending habits. Most lawyers simply adjust their lifestyles to their higher income levels anyway. Settling into a basic budgeting system now will develop the important habit of regular savings and investing, which are the basic materials for building a solid "financial house." Learning to balance out the fun you want to have today while addressing tomorrow's goals is the art of planning. The key is living an "accumulating" lifestyle, not a "consuming" one.

Too many lawyers also have a "preoccupation with the profession" where they feel compelled to maintain the image of being a lawyer. They buy into expensive new cars, large homes, fancy clothes, and Caribbean vacations, all of which drain away wealth. While they are busy impressing their clients and friends, they are depressing their net worth. Not only does excess spending thwart any realistic chance of reaching their larger, more important future financial goals, it also creates unnecessary yet self-inflicted financial stress.

Disorganization

Since lawyers are constantly facing challenges and deadlines for their clients, organizing materials relating to their own financial matters is rarely a priority. The problem is that disorganization hinders effective planning. Knowing where you are today is the very first step in being able to develop and manage a realistic financial plan.

Time spent looking for things simply costs you money. Lawyers are unfortunately too often directed by piles and files of paper everywhere. There is an inherent fear of losing something, so they keep everything. This clutter, however, causes distraction and confusion, and costly deadlines can be missed. From missing or underpaying income taxes owed to overlooking bank CD renewals or insurance policy rider deadlines, opportunities to save interest expenses, grow assets, or increase financial security are lost. The added stress caused by not knowing where you are also forces bad financial decisions like investing in things you already own. Productivity also decreases due to the time drain required to have to look for things buried in your "stuff." Too much momentum and energy is lost focusing on the stuff around you rather than the more important things you need to attend to like goals, planning, priorities, or people.

Getting organized pays high returns, because it results in more time and more knowledge. More time allows you to make better decisions, because you have all the facts easily in front of you to fully evaluate risks, rewards, costs, and benefits of a strategy or investment. You can avoid responding emotionally or being "sold to" by relentless agents when you have all the facts in front of you. Time also allows you to be more proactive taking advantage of financial opportunities rather than always stressfully reacting.

Speculation Versus Diversification

Too many lawyers have a net worth dominated by one or two large assets like their law practices, real estate, or their homes.

Because lawyers can understand complex financial details, they become more myopic in their focus and lose track of the overall picture of what is important in controlling their finances. They often take unnecessary risks based on unrealistic assumptions about the future instead of utilizing more prudent diversified strategies. Just because you understand all of the intricate details and assumptions of a complex investment deal does not mean you can control how it turns out.

However, just as a strong legal defense in a trial depends on the strength of more than one fact, so too should investment portfolios contain many asset types for weathering economic trials. Consider the New England real estate lawyer who, in a recent regional recession, saw his practice income as well as the value of his investment portfolio drop precipitously in one year because both were primarily based on commercial properties. If the lawyer needs to raise cash to pay bills until business picks up, the only option is to sell investments at the bottom of the market—a classic mistake brought on by poor diversification.

Lack of an Overall Plan or Direction

Too many lawyers do financial planning by crisis and not by design. They just react and too frequently move from one financial product to another with no integration. They make decisions based on convenience without incorporating all of their resources and goals into the decision-making process. Financial products may look good in and of themselves, but their merits should be weighed against your overall objectives, finances, and other strategies. Your unique planning goals should always dictate the financial products you invest in, not vice versa.

Other lawyers succumb to relentless insurance agents and stockbrokers who call them pitching the newest insurance plan or hot investment. Even if your insurance agent was a trusted college roommate, simply buying whole life and a mutual fund does not equal a comprehensive financial plan.

Financial products are just tools to be used to reach your goals, not ends in themselves. You don't need a product-focused agent; you want a trusted financial advisor who is planning-focused and more person-focused—on you. Avoid so-called "financial consultants" who tout the perfect financial product, because we have yet to find it.

The truth is that we all need to plan for our financial futures. The question is not whether to plan, but how to go about making a plan and whether we need a professional to help. Many lawyers hire a trusted financial advisor specifically to overcome these barriers. The right financial advisor will be your advocate, helping you to build a comprehensive plan that overcomes the barriers mentioned above to get the most out of your money. Financial advisors can charge fees on an hourly or flat fee basis, and some work solely for commissions on the products they manage for you. Most charge a combination of fees and commissions.

We are often asked, "How do you know who qualifies as a trusted financial advisor?" Look for the following characteristics:

Experience: They have practiced for a number of years and are not learning on your money. They have seen your concerns before and know how to solve them.

Expertise: They work with lawyers' finances and have the appropriate licenses in your state and credentials (such as being a certified financial planner™ professional).

Empathy: They are relationship-focused, they listen more than they talk, and they coach and encourage.

Energetic: They are able to keep up with your busy and changing life, they are proactive not reactive, they provide financial accountability, they are persistent enough to keep you on track but are not a pest, and they are disciplined enough to help you get things done.

Independence: They are planning-driven not product-directed, and they are not tied to one company's products or strategy.

Our experience has shown us that you will get what you "plan" for. Financial independence does not happen by accident; you have to be intentional and disciplined. Your money must work as hard as you do, and to do that you must have a plan. Too many lawyers unrealistically think they can just lead the good life, send their kids to private schools, and retire by age fifty-five. They do not have a realistic understanding of the skills, sacrifices, and strategies needed to make those goals a reality. Your plan needs to work no matter what, or it is just a bunch of dreams. The financial security of your family and your goals are far too important to be dependent upon just dreams or chance.

There is so much financial information out there, but sometimes not much wisdom. The purpose of this book is to show you how to plan and build solid strategies to overcome the barriers we see you facing so you can thrive financially. It summarizes the wisdom we have learned addressing issues that happen in real life—both good and bad—and have been shared with our lawyer clients throughout the years. *Real Life Financial Planning for Young Lawyers* is simply a practical method of organizing, understanding, and prioritizing financial decisions to help lawyers get their financial houses in order.

The case against lawyers building wealth is strong, but whether you hire an advisor or not, this book is your first step to entering your appeal to overcoming these barriers. You have such great potential as a lawyer to help others and to reach your own personal dreams and goals. If you can't see how yet, don't worry; just keep reading, because you're about to find out.

2

Where Should Lawyers
Start Building Wealth?

Building long-term financial security starts with making an honest assessment of where you are today. You have to have a plan and assess the "materials" you have to work with before building your "financial house."

Organizing Your Financial Files

The first financial tool is to develop an accessible organization system for all of your financial papers and personal information. In order to properly analyze your financial situation, make comparisons, and quickly review areas for possible changes, you need to have your financial data within easy reach. Think of it as if you are responding to a discovery request, gathering current, relevant information and organizing it correctly.

We recommend using a hanging file system held in a file cabinet (versus binders) with a separate one-third cut tab file for every set of important papers regarding your finances. Use a specific color file and hanging file—different than your office files—so you can easily identify your personal finance files no matter where you carry them.

Generally, place the files you will need to access more frequently in the beginning of your system and those less referenced towards the back. Use a numerical ordering system to number each file, and on the plastic tab/label place the reference number first, followed by the name describing what is in the file. For the major sections, start with 1000.00. For the next major section, use 1001.00, and so on. Each major section should be delineated by a clear plastic tab that sticks up from the hanging file. For each file in a subsection, use the numbers after the decimal point like 1005.01, 1005.02 on the tab/label on each file. Using a label printer helps to make these labels neater and easier to see.

Below is a sample listing of files using this system. (Hint: The sections and subsections will prompt you for some of the information you may need to collect.)

Sample Lawyers Personal Financial Filing System

1001.00   Financial Planning Information/Strategies to Review
1002.00   Net Worth Statements (Past and Present)
1003.00   Monthly Budget Records
1004.00   Family Personal Data
1005.00   Non-Qualified Investments
      1005.01   Stock/Bond/Mutual Fund Brokerage Account
      1005.02   Investment Real Estate
      1005.03   College Savings/529 Plans
      1005.04   Children's Gift (UTMA) Accounts
      1005.05   Variable (Non-Qualified) Annuity
1006.00   Qualified Investments
      1006.01   Law Firm Retirement Plan
      1006.02   Spouses Retirement Plan
      1006.03   ROTH IRA
      1006.04   Traditional IRA
1007.00   Pensions & Social Security
      1007.01   Pension Plan
      1007.02   Social Security Account Audits
1008.00   Insurance Policies
      1008.01   Homeowner's Insurance
      1008.02   Umbrella Liability Insurance
      1008.03   Professional Liability/Errors and Omissions
      1008.04   Auto Insurance
      1008.05   Health Insurance
      1008.06   Disability Income Insurance–Private
      1008.07   Group Disability Insurance
      1008.08   Life Insurance-Private
      1008.09 Life Insurance - Group
1009.00   Employee Benefits

Some of the above information can be kept electronically using programs available for budgeting, banking, and investing. You can also scan in other papers if you are technical enough to use a computer-based filing system.

You should also consider a fireproof home safe or bank safe deposit box for safeguarding car/home titles, original insurance policies, birth and marriage certificates, passports, wills, health care proxies, powers of attorney, social security cards, a videotape of your home contents, and a CD or tape backup of your computer files. Make copies of any of the contents you might need as a convenient working copy reference to place in your filing system.

Finally, it is important to use a shredder to destroy any papers you discard, especially those with social security, date of birth, or account numbers on them, to avoid identity theft.

Originating Your Model Monthly Budget

The vast majority of lawyers develop wealth by earning an income from their practice, spending just a portion of that income to live on today so they can save and invest the rest each month toward their future goals. A monthly budget system is simply a tool that can help you avoid spending more than you earn. The main purpose is to assist you in saving and investing regularly so you can grow assets.

Many budgeting systems exist ranging from simple paper forms to more complex computer-based programs. Use the system that works for you, the simpler the better. The first part of every budget system, though, is writing down all of your income and expenses for an average month. Use the Lawyers Model Budget Worksheet at the end of this chapter and fill in the average monthly amount you earn and spend in the various categories listed. Be thorough and break down all of the areas where you spend money in a given year into a monthly average. Feel free to add other areas where you spend if they do not appear on the worksheet. You may need to keep track of how you spend over a few months to get a more accurate idea of your real average expenses.

Once completed, this is your "model" budget, which shows you how, on average, you should be able to save, invest, reduce debt, and spend (SIRS) every month. The point of this exercise is that these numbers must all balance out—you cannot save, invest, reduce debt, and spend more than you make. You must save and invest some amount, no matter how small. If your expenses are more than your income, choose some expenses to reduce to make it balance out. If expenses are less than your income, increase the amounts you save and invest.

For some of you, this may feel like a tedious, dreadful process. If you had unlimited amounts of future income, there would be no need to budget. The fact is you have a limited supply of income, and therefore you have to apportion it in order to achieve your competing short- and long-term goals.

Think of this model budget as one of the blueprints in the overall plans for building your financial house. In Chapter 5, we will address further strategies to make your budgeting a more manageable process.

Outlining Your Net Worth Statement

You monthly budget represents a small moving picture of a part of your finances, whereas a net worth statement is a snapshot of how you are doing financially at a given point in time. A net worth statement consists of listing all of your assets and liabilities (or debts) and comparing the two. In simple terms, it is what you would be worth if you sold everything you owned and turned it into cash, then paid off all your debts. Your goal is to grow your net worth so your assets are far greater than your debts. Your net worth is an important way to keep score, and it measures much of your financial progress.

Many people measure their financial progress by how much money they have in the bank. In reality, as the value of such assets as a house, business, practice, or investments go up, and as you pay debts down, your net worth may be increasing more dramatically than you think.

Starting out in your career, your net worth may be negative thanks to large debts such as student loans. That is why it is so important for you to complete a current net worth statement now and sign and date it. Then, every year you can update it and compare it to prior years. This is a very motivating way to chart your progress. You will see yourself climb out of debt and watch your assets grow over time, making it a great reinforcement for you to continue to save and invest. A convenient time to do this is at the end of the year or when you are completing your income taxes.

Refer to the sample Net Worth Statement at the end of this chapter. There are several categories within a net worth statement.

Fixed assets is the first category. Fixed assets are those assets that have little or no risk of principal loss and usually include more conservative assets. A few examples would be bank checking and savings accounts, money mutual market funds, certificates of deposit, T-bills, EE savings bonds, and whole life insurance fixed cash values. These would be assets you have access to in an emergency—they are available now and so are considered liquid. Keep in mind, however, investments in a money market mutual fund are neither insured nor guaranteed by the FDIC or any government agency. Although the fund seeks to preserve the value of your investment at $1 per share, it is possible to lose money by investing in the fund.

Variable assets include most other financial assets. Examples include stocks, bonds, mutual funds, retirement plans, or any investment where the principal can fluctuate.

Your personal and other assets would include tangible assets like your house, personal or business property, and vehicles. Other tangible assets like stereos, computers, and cameras would also be included here.

Don't get too bogged down trying to establish a value for every piece of personal property. You may already have that information available from your homeowner's or renter's insurance policies, but if not, a rough estimate will work just fine. The main reason for gathering this information is to have an estimate so you can monitor trends. This way, when you are reviewing your net worth after some time, you will be able to track how this category has changed or account for some of the money you spent and invested.

For your **liabilities**, list the amount you owe if you could pay off the amount today, not the total of the payments over time, which would include interest. Don't forget to include all loans like mortgages, auto loans, credit cards, student loans, personal debts, and consumer debt.

Subtract your total liabilities from your assets to arrive at your net worth. For many people, this can be a sobering experience. Keep in mind that it is typical of young lawyers to have a negative net worth due to substantial student loans. However, your education is an investment in your financial future. Where else could you have invested $150,000 and expect a return of more than $100,000 for the next thirty years?

If you fit into the negative net worth category, your first financial goal is to get your net worth back to zero. This can be done by reducing debt and/or accumulating and/or growing assets. For you, it is especially important to establish a financial plan and get control of your financial life as soon as possible.

The Millionaire Next Door, by Dr. Thomas Stanley and William Danko, outlines some benchmark figures for what your net worth should be at any given time, age, or stage in life. Your net worth represents your financial security and, ultimately, your financial independence. So, of course, the closer you are to retirement, the higher your net worth should be. A successful financial plan—what we refer to as your financial house—achieves one's maximum net worth, works under all circumstances, and optimizes the enjoyment of your wealth.

In summary, being more organized with your financial data means it will be easier to stay on top of your planning and take advantage of financial opportunities and make the right changes more quickly. Budgeting so you can save, invest, reduce debt, and control spending each month can substantially build your net worth. Measuring your progress by annually recalculating and comparing your net worth helps to make sure you stay on track towards building a solid financial house.

In the remaining chapters, we will show you how to start building the financial house of your dreams.

NET WORTH STATEMENT

For: _____ As of: _____

Fixed Assets:

Savings Account	$15,000
Checking Account	$3,000
Certificate of Deposit	$2,000
Total Fixed Assets:	**$20,000**

Variable Assets:

IRA	$13,000
Roth IRA	$9,000
Mutual Funds	$10,000
Individual Stocks	$2,000
Variable Life Cash Value	$4,000
Law Practice	$45,000
401(k) Balance	$35,000
Total Variable Assets:	**$118,000**

Personal and Other Assets:

Home	$335,000
Vehicle	$20,000
Personal Property	$30,000
Total Personal and Other:	**$385,000**
Total Assets:	**$523,000**

Liabilities:

Mortgage	-$290,000
Home Equity Line of Credit	-$35,000
Vehicle Loan	-$10,000
Credit Cards	-$2,000
Student Loans	-$110,000
Total Liabilities:	**-$447,000**

Net Worth: Assets Minus Liabilities =   **$76,000**

Dated: _____ Signed: _____

Lawyers Model Budget Worksheet

Monthly Income Sources:

Income–Self: _____   Income–Spouse: _____

Bonuses: _____   Rental Income: _____

Other: _____   **TOTAL INCOME: $**[_____]

Monthly Expense Sources: (* = *Savings to Spend Expenses-see page 47*)

Fixed Expenses:	*Variable Expenses:*
Fed Taxes:	Food/Groceries:
State Taxes:	Clothes:
FICA Taxes:	Utilities-Gas
Mortgage/Rent:	Electricity:
Real Estate Taxes*:	Telephone:
Car Loan:	Cell Phone:
Credit Cards:	Water/Sewer*:
Student Loans:	Auto Gasoline:
Other Debts:	Auto Repairs:
Auto Insurance:	Household Help:
Home Insurance:	Medical Expenses:
Health Insurance:	New Home Purchases:
Disability Insurance:	Home Improvements:
Life Insurance:	Home Maintenance:
Other:	Education/Dues:
A. TOTAL FIXED EXP. $_____	Gifts/Birthdays*:
	Personal Care:
Saving/Investing:	Donations/Giving:
Bank Savings:	Newspapers/Magazines*:
Mutual Funds:	Allowances:
Debt Reduction:	Entertainment:
401(k) Plan:	Travel/Vacations*:
Other:	Cable TV:
Other:	Other:
B. TOTAL SAVING /	Other:
INVESTING $_____	Other:
Compare Total Income (above)	C. TOTAL VARIABLE
to Expenses (below):	EXPENSES: $_____
Total Income less	TOTAL EXPENSES + Saving:
Total Expenses less	= A + B + C
Total Savings/Investing	$_____
MUST equal $0!	

3

Getting Your Financial House in Order

Just gathering the financial "materials" you have available like your net worth, budget, and other financial data will not automatically build the wealth you desire. You have to make all that you have integrate together in the most efficient ways possible to build the picture of your finances you want. Our clients hire us as their "financial architects" to help them put it all together through the method of a financial plan. Like the blueprints to follow in building a home, a financial plan takes the materials you have and draws up pictures of how you can fit everything together to build the wealth you want. We designed the concept of your financial house as a method of seeing how a properly designed financial plan looks when it is put together correctly.

The financial house is a simple and easy-to-remember method of explaining real financial planning concepts by categorizing your financial plan into levels like the floors of a house. If you want your house to stand solidly, it must be built in a certain logical sequence of levels—from the bottom up. The same is true for your financial house. No matter what your financial house looks like on the surface, there are basic internal construction processes you must use to prevent it from collapsing.

For example, you start by laying the foundation level, then add on the various levels. The more solid the foundation, the bigger the structure it can support. Then, brick by brick, piece by piece, additional layers are added to form the house. A solid financial plan must be built in the same way with materials, strategies, and tools properly applied in the right priority and order. Financial success isn't, as many people believe, the ability to make one or two decisions through a get-rich-quick scheme that turns a buck into a million dollars. Rather, financial success is the result of many small but sound decisions that, when compounded, add up to substantial financial security.

Your financial house also must be just as solid as your regular home, because there is so much "bad weather" coming against your ability to build and maintain it. Not only do lawyers face their own specific internal barriers to accumulating wealth, but that wealth needs to be protected from the many external forces that can deplete, damage, or even demolish their ability to keep it. Those forces might be the normal winds of change in your life like getting married, having a child, or changing jobs. Others could be the unpredictable storms of emergencies you may face, like unexpected home repairs or the sudden loss of a spouse. Still others are the everyday weather patterns of ever-rising taxes, growing inflation, investment risks, and changing interest rates. If your financial house is improperly designed, money that should be accumulating will fly out the window to pay for these expenses. You have to make sure your financial house can withstand your next financial hurricane.

Your financial house must also be flexible enough to anticipate the sunny days when opportunities come so you can take advantage of them. Funding your Roth IRA or 401(k), buying in as partner in the firm, a real estate deal, or even a new home require you to plan ahead and have the cash available to do these things. You will need to position your finances to participate in these opportunities when they arise.

A successful financial plan is like a weather-resistant home—no weather pattern can impact its structural integrity. It works no matter what weather comes against it—good or bad. It should also help you enjoy your money as a tool to reach your goals and maximize the growth of your net worth.

YOUR FINANCIAL HOUSE PLAN

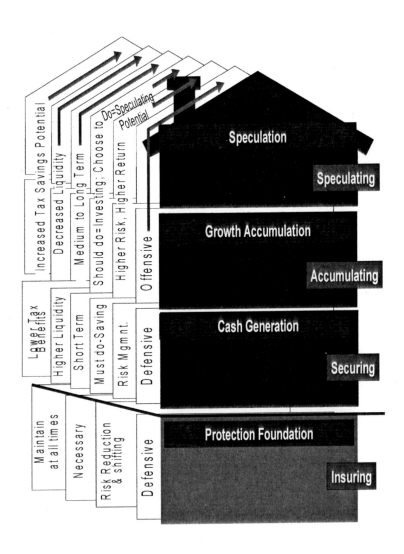

We sometimes refer to the financial house as a picture of your total net worth or wealth as well. There is more motivation now than ever before to save and invest, because it is looking like you will need to be building more of a financial mansion than a house. People are living much longer than expected, medical and college costs are soaring, retirement benefits are being cut, and inevitable social "insecurity" changes mean your financial house needs to be built much bigger than you may realize, or you will never be able to completely retire. You need to build your wealth now so you can have something to live in and live off of later.

As you can see by the picture on the previous page, there are four main levels to building your financial house.

The Protection Foundation Level

Before you go on the offensive and begin risking money to grow your financial house, you need to first do all you can to reduce those risks that could seriously undermine your wealth-building goals. The most cost-effective way to reduce or shift risk is to buy professionally designed insurance protection. You need to insure against losing what you have accumulated, what you will accumulate, and against others or events taking it away.

This first level of protection foundation is the most important and should be done first, because all the other levels rely on it like the floors of a house must rest on the foundation. Without the security of the foundation being sturdy, walls and floors will shift and crack and overall structural integrity is compromised. The opposite strategy is self-insuring, which can also lead to problems. Your assets could easily be wiped out as they are used to fund the cost of these catastrophic events. Without proper layers of insurance protection put down first, your financial house rests on shifting sand—a false sense of security that "that won't ever happen to me."

As a lawyer, you know people are sued every day. They can die prematurely, get in costly car accidents, and lose their homes. Many times, these events occur without adequate insurance to pay for the unplanned event, forcing them to liquidate their wealth. Countless times, we have seen lawyers who knew better faced with liquidating their own assets to address something they could have insured for and been protected from.

Your first financial priority should not be on growing assets and tax strategies but on security. Insurance is necessary and should be maintained at all times.

The Cash Generation Level

Now you can focus on the primary method of building up wealth, and that is generating cash from your income to save, invest, and reduce debts through your monthly budget. Whatever budget system you use, it must help you to spend less so you can commit a monthly amount to save, first building emergency reserves and reducing high-interest debts.

Although this is still a defensive strategy, emergency funds act as "insurance," so you will not be forced to sell off wealth-building growth investments for needed cash. This strategy is investing for a short-term time frame in low-risk, very accessible, liquid accounts like bank savings accounts, which allows you to "self-manage" many of the smaller emergencies you face. Paying off debt simply saves loan interest expense, which is a form of "guaranteed" return. Any additional amount you can set aside can then be used to invest for the medium and long term in Growth Accumulation Level (see Chapter 6) strategies. You must start saving right out of law school as soon as possible to get this important habit developed.

The Growth Accumulation Level

This next level allows you to take risk by accumulating and compounding capital through investments. Your goal now is to be offensive yet with risk you are comfortable with, in an attempt to achieve much higher potential returns than more secure savings vehicles. Although you can face daily fluctuations in the value of these investments, you are investing now for medium- to long-term holding periods and don't need to use this money in the short run. Example accumulation vehicles are stocks, bonds, mutual funds, annuities, cash value life insurance, real estate, college savings programs, IRAs, Roth IRAs, and employer-sponsored retirement plans like 401(k)s.

Many investments also have tax savings potential, but for those tax advantages, you often have to give up access to the money. There is generally no long-term investment that is also a good short-term investment. If you are forced to quickly liquidate many of these vehicles, the risk of principal loss, taxes, penalties, and potential loss of growth can be very costly. This makes learning how to diversify investments critical to long-term wealth-building.

Almost everyone should take some risk to accumulate capital just to outpace inflation, but do not jump into investments without a strategy and a plan, because there are no guaranteed returns in growth-oriented investments.

The Aggressive Growth Speculation Level

Now that you have properly insured against catastrophic losses, can live within your means, and have invested prudently to accumulate assets, you can afford to speculate with some of your money in an attempt to achieve even higher returns. Investments here have the highest potential for loss and are often illiquid (can't be sold for cash in a short time frame). There can be potential tax savings as well through these vehicles. Risk only the capital you can afford to lose. For many, that amount would be zero and they should avoid the speculation level entirely and instead choose to build up more assets at the other levels.

As your financial architects, we have now given you the framework to build your financial house. Its power is that it will help you focus on what is important in the proper structuring of your house. Let's use the materials you have collected in Chapter 2 and apply some tools together with appropriate strategies and start building your house.

4

The Protection Foundation Level

The first step to building wealth is to be defensive and lay a firm foundation of insurance protection. A solid financial plan considers the fact that many times in life things do not go as planned. Insurance protection is how you plan for unforeseen catastrophic losses. These losses could create such a hole that, without insurance, you may never dig yourself out. Insurance is necessary and should be maintained at all times. These insurance coverages are auto, homeowner's/renter's, personal umbrella liability, professional malpractice, disability income, disability buyout, business overhead, health, long-term care, and life.

The strategy here is to shift these large risks to insurance carriers in exchange for much smaller premium payments. This allows you to invest most of your money more aggressively elsewhere, compounding it for a longer period of time since you know you are protected from having to touch it at an inappropriate time like when the markets are down or when you would have to pay penalties and taxes for using it.

For a moment, imagine a world without any insurance. You would have to put all of your assets in a safe, more liquid area like a bank, because you never know when you would have to use it to pay cash for all of your medical expenses, car accidents, lost wages, and so on. You cannot afford to leave all your cash in the bank and earn low interest rates on it (lower risk, lower return potential) and expose it to the erosion of inflation and income taxes. This would be a slow road to wealth that wouldn't get you there in your lifetime.

As a lawyer, you must realize that you also have a lot to lose today and in the future. Although you may not have a lot of assets at this point, you will, and your future earnings are actually your greatest asset. For example, a thirty-year-old lawyer earning $100,000 a year has a future earnings potential of over $9 million with just a 5 percent annual increase in earnings. The time to obtain insurance protection is always before the loss occurs; you cannot obtain it after. Planning, after all, is about preparation and avoiding oversights. If you are underinsured, the difference will deplete your savings or even your future earnings to make up the difference.

Liability and Asset Protection

Most lawyers won't practice without professional malpractice coverage, which is mostly provided for them through their firms. Those same lawyers, however, rarely have adequate personal liability coverage on their auto or homeowner's insurance plans. The limits built into most homeowner's and auto policies are minimal. These coverages are too often "sold" based on the cheapest premiums rather than on what coverage design can provide the maximum security to your financial plan.

This coverage part of your auto and homeowner's/renter's policies actually protects you and your assets in the event you or a family member cause harm due to negligence. You are also protected if negligence occurs on your property. In addition, be sure to ask your agent for excess liability coverage for uninsured/underinsured motorists. This coverage protects you and your family for negligent acts caused by others. You should also secure a separate personal umbrella liability policy for at least $1 million that is added on top of your auto and homeowner's/renter's policies. We think you should strongly consider obtaining the maximum protection you can from these policies and manage the premium cost with higher deductibles.

You should also review your overall financial plan to see what assets are at risk in the event of a lawsuit. As a lawyer, you know we live in a society where successful and wealthy people are targeted for lawsuits more than other groups. In the event of a lawsuit due to an accident on your property, it is important to know what assets could be subject to creditors if the judgment is over your insurance limits. Each state has different laws regarding protected assets. Some examples of assets that are protected in certain states are a personal residence, qualified retirement plans, IRAs, cash value life insurance, annuities, or cars. Keep in mind that these vary from state to state. You should talk with your trusted advisor to see how your state views various assets or do your own legal research with a litigation colleague. You can limit your risk by insuring properly and knowing the rules of protected assets in your state.

Income Protection: Disability Income Insurance

When you break down a financial plan and the desire to become financially independent, your income and savings level will determine your success. If your ability to earn an income is interrupted, the plan will fall apart quickly unless you protect yourself. In fact, for most young lawyers your income is what your entire plan is based on, so you must protect that income as a primary strategy.

The odds of a long-term disability occurring (lasting ninety days or longer) are six to seven times greater than a death during your working years. Financially, a long-term disability is very costly since your expenses still need to be paid and continue to rise over time. Early in your career, the only way to guarantee your income will not stop is to insure yourself with a private occupation-specific disability insurance policy. Occupation-specific means if you cannot perform the duties of your regular occupation as a lawyer, you will be compensated.

You will want to secure disability coverage as soon as possible, because policies are priced based on age, health, and the amount of benefits you buy. The younger you are, the cheaper the policy will be. The premiums can also be fixed for the length of the policy, which is usually to age sixty-seven. Before you face any health issues, the coverage will also be approved more easily. Utilize insurance carriers who have quality contract features that favor lawyers and even those who will issue contracts to you in your last year of law school.

Other important features to make sure you include in your policy are the following:

Residual Disability Benefit: This option ensures that if your injury or illness limits your ability to practice only partially, the policy will pay a partial or proportionate benefit. Without this option, the policy only pays if you are totally disabled from your occupation.

Guaranteed Renewal/Non-Cancelable Policy: Once the policy has been issued, the company cannot change your rate or cancel the policy. It is a unilateral contract, meaning only you can make a change to the policy.

Future Purchase Option: This option allows you to add coverage to your policy in the future without medical underwriting. With disability insurance being quite difficult to obtain due to stringent underwriting, this is particularly important. The following are some examples of issues that can make it difficult to obtain or increase a personal policy in the future as you age:

- History of mental/nervous/stress counseling
- Diabetes
- Excessive speeding tickets/DWI
- Back pain, chiropractic concerns
- Elevated liver enzymes
- Above-average weight

Inflation Protection: This option provides that once you receive benefits, the monthly benefit will increase with inflation. Over twenty-five years, at only 3 percent inflation, a $200,000 income will need to grow to $418,000 to have the same purchasing power, and that increase needs to be protected.

Disability insurance is not an exciting area of planning, but until you have accumulated enough money to retire, it is one of the most important fundamental financial considerations. A disability policy will keep your financial life in order in the event of a disability, but the premiums should not significantly impact your ability to save for the future.

It is also typical for many law practices to provide group disability coverage for you. Group plans, however, have many contractual limitations. They typically will cover only about 60 percent of your income. If the firm pays the premium for you as an employee and deducts the cost as a business expense, the benefit paid by the group policy to you when you have a claim will be considered taxable income to you. The result is a net after-tax benefit equivalent to only 40 to 45 percent of your pre-disability income. Group plans are also not portable, so when you leave the firm, you also lose the coverage. Lawyers should not overly rely on law firm group disability benefits, because they do change firms frequently and will need more than 40 percent of their income protected. Plan to supplement your group disability plan with a private individual disability policy.

Remember, you get what you pay for. Searching the Internet for the cheapest insurance policy often results in coverage that will not protect you and your family adequately. A competent insurance agent or financial planner can provide a valuable service and should be used. They can be the best resource in helping you professionally select and design coverage at a reasonable cost. At claim time as well they can help you decipher the paperwork. Choosing someone you trust, especially someone who comes recommended from a reliable source, will prove invaluable.

Income Protection: Business Overhead Expense

If you are in a small or solo practice and are unable to work for an extended period of time, the effect on your practice can be devastating. You should review your situation to see if your practice could withstand the loss of revenue you or your partners generate. If the loss of the revenue would result in financial difficulty, it is advisable to purchase a business overhead expense policy.

According to the Health Insurance Association of America, 30 percent of all people between ages thirty-five and sixty-five will suffer a disability of at least ninety days. About one in seven can expect to become disabled for five years or more. The average duration of a disability lasting more than ninety days, beginning prior to age sixty-five, is four years and four months for ages forty to forty-four, four years and seven months for ages forty-five to forty-nine, and four years and six months for ages fifty to fifty-four.

These policies pay the overhead of your practice if you or a partner is disabled and are deductible as a business expense. Most policies begin to pay in thirty, sixty, or ninety days with the shorter waiting period being more expensive. The policy should cover the amount of overhead you are responsible for. Some insurance companies will limit the amount of coverage you can apply for to $25,000 per month.

Expenses normally considered as business expenses would include the following:

- Compensation and employer-paid benefits
- Salary of a non-family member hired to replace you
- Rent and lease payments
- Utility costs
- Maintenance and service
- Legal and accounting fees
- Property insurance
- Liability insurance
- Malpractice insurance
- Business insurance
- Professional dues
- Business debt and interest
- Business property taxes
- Supplies
- Postage

You should also select a benefit period that matches your situation. The benefit period sets the number of months the policy will pay. The most common benefit periods are twelve, eighteen, or twenty-four months.

If you are starting a practice or expect your practice to grow, you should add a future increase option to your policy. This option allows you to add more coverage to your policy without having to answer any medical questions. The increase is subject to financial review only.

Make sure the policy will pay if you cannot perform the material duties of your occupation as a lawyer. A policy that pays if you cannot do any occupation is not acceptable. You can also add additional options to the policy like the residual disability rider. This option assures that the policy will pay if you are partially disabled but still able to perform limited duties.

Income Protection: Disability Buyout Insurance

Another type of income protection important to law partners in a partnership is called a disability buyout policy. It provides a lump sum to your law partner(s) or the practice in the event of a long-term disability to you or your partner(s). This will ensure that the disabled partner receives a timely buyout and provides the necessary liquidity to the practice to buy out the disabled partner. Many practices insure the buyout at the death of a partner with life insurance but do not consider the impact of a partner that is disabled and can no longer practice or generate revenue. Financially, the impact is just as significant. Statistically, a male age thirty-five to fifty-five is almost twice as likely to become disabled than die, and a female age thirty-five to fifty-five is nearly three times as likely to become disabled.

As the group grows in size, the odds of a disability among partners increases, but size of the assets to buffer the shock to the group should also grow. See the chart below showing the probability of at least one long-term disability prior to age sixty-five.

| Age | Number of Owners | | | | |
	2 lives	3 lives	4 lives	5 lives	6 lives
25	36.5%	49.4%	59.7%	67.8%	74.4%
35	34.2%	46.7%	56.7%	64.9%	71.5%
45	31.1%	42.8%	52.5%	60.6%	67.3%
55	23.4%	33%	41.4%	48.7%	55.1%

As the group grows to ten or more, the odds are over 90 percent that one partner will be disabled for ninety days or longer. (Source: 1985 Society of Actuaries DSP Experience Tables)

Buyout policies have a waiting period that requires the disability to last a specified period of time before paying the lump sum. The most common waiting periods are one year, eighteen months, or two years. The waiting period also prevents a buyout from occurring too soon. It should be fairly clear after eighteen months if the disabled partner is recovering and whether the buyout should happen.

Practice Continuation Planning

We find most law partners have an understanding of the basics of structuring a business continuation plan for their practice. In the agreement, the partners will typically specify what will happen in the event of a death, disability, or termination of one of the partners. Normally, the partners will mutually agree to buy out the deceased, disabled, or departing partner's interest for a specified value based on a formula. It is important to update the valuation periodically.

The untimely passing, disability, retirement, or termination of a partner can present significant financial challenges. Without a well-designed strategy, there can be conflicts between the remaining owners and departed owners or heirs relating to distribution of income and the sale of the practice. In the event of death or disability in a professional corporation, it is very important to have this structured properly due to the limitations that limit ownership to licensed practitioners only.

Although very capable of drafting these shareholder arrangements, too many law firms either do not implement them or have them but have not actually funded them. Funding is critical, because it is often difficult for the remaining owner(s) to quickly come up with the funds to buy out the departed partner's interest. A well-designed business continuation plan will provide funding for the deceased, disabled, terminated, or retired partner's share of the practice. This can be done through the use of insurance or savings. The best way to guarantee that money will be available is to have life insurance and disability buyout insurance in place on all the partners sufficient to cover the buyout. Also, requiring partners to carry private and group disability income insurance will provide income for them once they are bought out.

In the event of death, the most common types of funding arrangements are the stock redemption and cross-purchase strategies. The following briefly summarizes each option:

Stock Redemption

- Corporation is the owner and beneficiary of the life insurance.
- The cost of the policies is spread among the shareholders.
- If you are using permanent life policies, the cash values are subject to corporate creditors.
- Only one policy per shareholder is required, which is advantageous for firms with a large number of partners.
- The death benefit may be subject to the alternative minimum tax.

Cross-Purchase

- Shareholders own and are the beneficiaries of the life insurance policies on their partners.
- The cost of insurance is higher for younger shareholders who pay for policies on the older partners.
- Cash values are subject to the shareholders' creditors in most states if you are using permanent policies.
- The death benefit is not subject to the alternative minimum tax.

For larger law groups, it is common to use the stock redemption strategy, and in practices with three or fewer owners, a cross-purchase plan can work well.

If you or your partner(s) plan to work until a normal retirement age, you should also address other issues like:

- How will the practice buy out the retiring partners?
- What will the retiring partner do about life and health insurance?
- How will the tail malpractice coverage be handled?

A well-designed business continuation plan will help facilitate and fund the sale of your practice in the event of a premature death or disability and in the event of a long and healthy life.

Life Insurance Protection

When it comes to life insurance, it is easy to become confused. Complicated terminology like "term life," "whole life," "universal life," "variable whole life," and so on may put you off, but by understanding just a few terms and some of the benefits and disadvantages, you will be much better prepared to evaluate the best coverage for you. If structured correctly, life insurance can be one of the most versatile and powerful financial tools available, and it should not be overlooked.

Life insurance has many uses. The simplest to understand is the desire to protect the ones you care about in the event of your untimely death. Additional uses are to:

- Protect your family's financial security by replacing your lost income
- Secure a loan to buy a practice
- Accumulate and protect wealth (permanent life policies only)
- Pay estate taxes
- Draw more income from your retirement assets without the fear of leaving nothing to your heirs
- Provide liquid dollars in the event of the untimely death of a business partner

Focusing on the simplest desire for coverage to protect the ones you care about in the event of your untimely death, it is important to understand how the policy works and how much death benefit to obtain. Life insurance benefits are stated in a specific lump sum. For example, a $1,000,000 policy would pay $1,000,000 to the stated beneficiary upon death of the insured free of income taxes.

Since your income terminates at your death, it would be advisable to provide for a lump sum that, if properly invested, could continue paying an income to your family. In other words, when you die, your family loses your future potential income at your death. For example, if you make $200,000 annually and you die tomorrow and want to continue your $200,000 income indefinitely to your family, you should secure about $4 million in life insurance. The $4,000,000 would be payable **income tax-free** to your family. If the lump sum is invested at 5 percent interest, your family could draw $200,000 per year of **taxable income** without depleting the principal. It is wise to use a conservative investment return on death benefit proceeds, as beneficiaries will most likely be very conservative with managing the insurance money. This simple analysis does not factor in potential social security benefits, the long-term effects of inflation, or limits on what insurance companies are willing to issue you.

Life insurance is one of the only insurance coverages with which people generally don't think about insuring the loss for its full replacement value. If your $500,000 home burned down, would you want it replaced with a $200,000 home? No. If your $200,000 income is lost to your family, do you want to replace it with a $50,000 income, $100,000 income, or the full replacement of $200,000? Generally, most people would want to insure for full replacement value. The amount of life insurance you should own then is the amount you would buy today if you knew you were going to die tomorrow. Our litigation lawyer clients have taught us that the amount you should be insured for is what your heirs would sue for if you died in a wrongful death situation. In most court cases, that amount is the full replacement value of the deceased's lost earnings. Think of life insurance as the cornerstone of your financial house, for it protects your income, assets, and those you love the most.

Types of Life Insurance

There are two broad types of life insurance: term and permanent. To understand the difference, it is helpful to compare term insurance to renting an apartment and permanent life insurance to owning a home. Term insurance is inexpensive when you are young, but the cost increases exponentially as you age. You can buy a term policy where the premium goes up every year or stays level for five, ten, twenty, or thirty years. Term insurance provides a large amount of temporary coverage at a low cost for young, healthy people. It will always terminate at some point in the future and offers few living benefits or equity.

Right out of law school, it is advisable to obtain a supplemental private term life policy to guarantee your insurability. You will want to lock the coverage in now, because it is cheap at younger ages and because your health now will most likely get you the best rating. The cost for $1,000,000 of term insurance is between $25 and $55 per month, so protecting your insurability and your family is quite affordable. Your term policy should be convertible to a permanent policy without medical underwriting. This conversion feature guarantees that if your health changes, you do not need to worry about re-qualifying for the coverage after the initial term. So, be sure the company you purchase your term insurance from has competitive permanent policies to convert to and is highly rated for its financial soundness. Do not rely on your law firm's group term life insurance, as you lose it if you leave the firm.

As a long-term strategy, some lawyers try buying term insurance and taking the difference in premiums between the term and permanent policy and investing it in mutual funds. This can be an effective strategy if you **always** maintain the discipline to invest the difference on a monthly basis and are sure you will not want life insurance later in life. Very few people can save without interruption for forty years, and with life expectancies increasing, having at least some permanent life insurance is becoming a necessity.

Even if you could save over the course of twenty or more years, the tax implications of this strategy unravels its effectiveness. The tax inefficiencies increase as you near retirement, because many lawyers reallocate their portfolios as they become more conservative as they get older. This requires owning more income-producing investments that are taxable like bond funds. To accomplish this, you may have to pay capital gains taxes when you sell your stock funds to buy these bond funds. Bonds also generate ordinary income, which for highly compensated lawyers will be at a higher tax rate than the capital gain and dividend distributions from your stock portfolio. Taxes are owed annually on this strategy, because most lawyers will have exhausted their tax-deferred investment options like IRAs, SEPs, or 401(k) profit-sharing plans. This leaves only taxable accounts to invest the difference in premiums between the term and permanent policy.

Permanent life policies are designed to be in force for your entire life. They generally have a fixed premium with a portion of the premium allocated to a tax-deferred account (often called "cash value") and a portion to the cost of the policy. This is similar to a mortgage payment where some of your payment pays interest and some principal.

The tax-deferred account builds equity and either pays you a fixed percentage or allows you to direct your money across a wide range of conservative to aggressive sub-accounts. Permanent policies are designed to last as long as you do and can even reach "paid up" status, requiring no more premium contributions. (For many people, some permanent life policies may be too expensive.)

Lawyers often have higher incomes, placing them in a high income tax bracket. So, a permanent life policy can be a good long-term financial strategy. This is especially true if you meet the following criteria:

- You have a need for life insurance.
- You are phased out of contributing to a Roth IRA.
- You are funding at the maximum level your current retirement plan (i.e. your 401(k)).
- You have a significant net worth now or will have by retirement.
- You have additional discretionary dollars that can be used for long-term financial security.
- You are looking for additional ways to defer investment income from tax.

A sound strategy is to fund a life policy right at or just under the modified endowment limits. This maximizes the accumulation portion compared to the insurance expenses. You want to avoid having your policy become a modified endowment contract, because cash value withdrawals can be income taxed and penalized.

There are many types of permanent life insurance. It is advisable to make sure the kind you are considering is designed for your intended use whether it be family protection, estate planning, business continuation, or supplemental retirement income. This is one of the most complex financial products in the marketplace, so be sure you work with a competent, knowledgeable, and experienced advisor.

Basic Estate Planning for Young Lawyers

As a young lawyer, the last thing on your mind is the thought of dying prematurely. However, if you are taking our protection level planning to heart, you will have a substantial estate right away through the life insurance protection you own. Therefore, you should be careful to designate the beneficiaries on your policies (including any law firm group term life and retirement plans), and you may want to have at least a simple will drafted by a qualified estate planning colleague you trust. More importantly, have powers of attorney implemented in addition to designating someone to act on your behalf for financial or medical decisions if you are incapacitated. The odds of a sickness affecting you are far greater than death. So many of you can have these documents implemented for free or even do them yourself through your own law firm. The first step is to just get them completed for now. You will spend a lifetime revising them.

In many cases, insurance is thought of as a "necessary evil." You have to have it, but it only benefits you if you have a claim. You need to see that the properly structured insurance coverage can be a valuable part of an overall comprehensive financial plan. Insurance enhances the use of your other assets. The comfort you have by knowing you and your family are covered is also worth a lot. In addition, you can more aggressively spend and invest, because you know your risk management needs are taken care of.

Looking back to the Middle Ages, you can get a glimpse of the importance of insurance. People of wealth built fabulous castles and filled them with treasures. They always devoted significant resources to protecting those assets in the form of an army, a moat, and so on. In a sense, that was an early form of an insurance policy. So, as you continue to build your net worth, you should review and update your insurance to be sure you are maximizing your coverage and protecting yourself, your family, and your wealth.

5

The Cash Generation Level

This may be the most important part of this book for you as a young lawyer, because now you are forming key spending habits and financial attitudes. You must realize that they can either serve you or you will serve them the rest of your life. One of the most critical financial habits is living within your means. Put another way, you should not spend more than you earn, since this only creates debt. You should spend less than what you earn so you can save and invest the difference to build a bigger financial house. As basic as this strategy sounds, we find it to be one of the most difficult financial habits for most lawyers to put into practice.

Why is something that is so easily understood and readily agreed upon by lawyers so difficult for them to follow? A primary reason is that too many lawyers do not practice regular budgeting habits to help them regularly build wealth through regular saving and investing. Secondly, there are some key problems that undermine budgeting systems that must be negated with effective processes to make budgeting work in reality.

Start Turning Income into Wealth

Your first step in getting a hold on your cash flow is to make sure you have filled out your Model Budget Worksheet back in Chapter 2. This is your plan for how your cash flow should work each month. You need to get an overall picture of what your monthly income is and compare it to the average monthly expenses you have. Be sure to include all the areas in which you spend money. Fixed expenses are those that are the same amount each month, and variable are those that may vary. To get a good idea of your expenses, you may need to carry around a pocket calendar for a month or two and write down what you spend. You should add a "miscellaneous expense" amount that reflects the little variable expenses that seem to come up each month. These expenses individually are not significant, but added together they can be quite large. Examples of these are veterinary bills, household items, lunches out, coffee, diapers, and so on. Then, target a monthly savings and investing figure that should start at a minimum of 1 percent but ideally be closer to 20 percent of your gross income.

You then reconcile your model budget with a goal that your cash flow must balance out according to the following formula:

> Total Income
> Less: Total Fixed Expenses (A)
> Less: Total Saving/Investing (C)
> Less: Total Variable Expenses (B)
> = Zero dollars!

If the above calculation results in higher than zero, you should increase what you can save and invest. If the above results in a negative number, you need to reduce your expenses—not your saving and investing—to make the formula balance out back to zero. The whole purpose of any budget process is primarily to generate cash for saving and investing. You have to come to terms with spending at a level that addresses what you need today yet is below you buying everything you want. The saving and investing will help you build up the wealth to still get what you want over time.

Why Is It So Hard to Actually Live by the Model Budget You Created?

Use a "savings to spend" account to tackle irregular expenses.

One problem we see that undermines budgeting is that you have too many expenses that come up at irregular times—other than monthly—that cause you to overspend when they are due. They may be expenses like car insurance that is paid quarterly, water bills that come semiannually, or seasonal gift-giving like Christmas, birthdays, or anniversaries. Each of these should be a listed expense in your model budget, and you should make note of them with an asterisk. The dollar amount you record for them in your model budget should be the monthly amount required to be set aside to pay them when they are due.

The important thing is to look over a whole calendar year to identify your irregular expenses, recognize when they come due, and define what they each should cost. Then, add up all these irregular expenses into one annual total. Divide this total by twelve to get the monthly average of all your irregular bills. The key to this system is to set aside that amount each month in what we call a "savings to spend" savings account. This is a separate savings account you escrow the money into each month to pay these bills from when they come due. If set up at the same bank where you have your personal checking, it is easier to transfer funds from savings to checking to pay the irregular bills.

This is just a way to make these irregular bills a regular, planned-for occurrence so that every month your expenses are more consistent. The point is, if you give it some thought, you can anticipate when these expenses occur each year. By thinking about them ahead of time (planning), you also have to budget an amount to spend on them so they do not surprise you (reacting) and force you to spend more that month. See the "Savings to Spend" Account Expense Worksheet at the end of the chapter to help you develop your system.

Pay your bills systematically to make budgeting a habit.

A second problem we see that prevents a model budget from being followed is the sporadic way many lawyers pay their bills. If you can establish a system to pay your bills at the same time, in the same way, and even in the same order each month, you will have a better chance of controlling your cash flow. Again, you are trying to take the irregularity out of your cash flow with systems that help you control things by making them the same or habitual every month.

A priority payment system could look like this:

1. First, set aside monthly savings and investing amounts before you pay your bills. This "paying your self first" habit can be implemented more easily if you use automatic investment plans,

which remove money electronically from your checking account or your paycheck and send it to an investment or savings account.

2.   Second, pay all of your fixed expenses next. Pay them in the order they are due. Anytime you can automate bill paying, take advantage of it to form this habit. This can be done through various online banking functions, and many bills offer to automatically deduct what you owe them each month right from your checkbook.

3.   Third, set aside the monthly "savings to spend" amount into your "savings to spend" account. Again, you could have this amount electronically transferred on the same date each month from your checking account or paycheck into this savings account to make it like a regular "bill."

4.   Fourth, pay your irregular bills that come due that month from the money you have escrowed in your "savings to spend" account. A simple transfer from the savings account back to checking, so the bill can be paid, makes this easy to implement.

All of the above steps should be done in the same order for the same amounts each month. This process leaves just enough money in your checkbook to cover the remaining variable expenses you have to pay each month. These steps are self-induced "financial controls" that force you to live within the remaining cash you have left. Also, what you don't have available—because you have used it in Steps 1 through 4—you cannot spend.

Reset income tax withholding to increase cash flow.

A third problem that prevents model budgets from balancing in reality is that too many lawyers inadequately address their annual income taxes. The vast majority receive larger-than-necessary annual income tax refunds that could be much better used to build wealth each month if it was saved or invested. In effect, they loan their hard-earned money to the U.S. government at 0 percent interest for over a year. They also miss the investment return they could have earned on that money and often pay high credit card interest that could have been avoided. Even if you are a terrible saver and are overpaying your taxes as a forced savings plan, we see this backfiring more often than not because most will just spend the tax refund on something!

The best way to estimate the taxes you owe is to complete an income tax projection for each tax year. We encourage you to do this working with your accountant, running one of the many tax software packages available, or simply using the Basic Federal Tax Estimator included at the end of this chapter. This is a basic guide only for education purposes, and it doesn't factor in all of the specifics of your tax situation like tax credits, phase-outs, student loan interest deductions, moving expenses, and so on. But it can help to get an approximate estimate of your federal tax liability.

All you do is plug in your income sources (wages, interest, capital gains, etc.) and subtract adjustments to income (IRAs, retirement contributions, etc.) to get your adjusted gross income. From that, you subtract your personal exemptions and either the standard deduction or your itemized deductions, whichever is higher. The result is the taxable income you use— along with the tax rate chart—to calculate the total federal taxes you owe this year. You should also estimate your state taxes if you live in a state with state income taxes. As your income and/or deductions increase, you may become subject to the alternative minimum tax (AMT). You should review this issue if it arises with a qualified tax professional.

The most important part of this exercise is to divide the total taxes you owe by the number of paychecks you receive in a year to get your per-paycheck estimated tax amount. Then compare the per-paycheck estimated tax with what taxes you currently have taken out of each of your paychecks. Most lawyers need to reduce what they have taken out, and a reduction in taxes withheld results in an increase in their paychecks that they can save and invest. The way to make this change is through your employer's payroll department by filling out a new W-4 form.

You especially need to reset your paycheck tax withholding if you are graduating in May or June and starting employment mid-year. If you don't set the proper tax withholding, employer payroll systems tend to take out higher taxes since they assume you were earning your full salary for the entire year. There are enough new expenses you need to address starting a new job that could be more easily paid for with a higher take-home pay now than getting a tax refund the following spring. You also can more easily begin your saving and investing program right away with your first paycheck.

You also need to complete a tax projection to reset your tax withholding if you have a major change in your life that will affect your taxes. Family changes like a birth, death, or marriage all affect the tax you owe. Financial changes such as a new job, raise, becoming a partner in your firm, going back to school, or buying or moving to a new house can also impact your tax liability, and a new calculation with adjustments should be made.

In any event, we suggest you estimate your tax liability in advance and try to end up about even—paying what you owe each month and no more. This also avoids any under-withholding penalties and any unexpected tax liability due that you may not be prepared for.

We sometimes hear lawyers who lament about the large amount of taxes they pay when they tell us, "I just got a raise (or a bonus, or a large contingency fee), and it jumped me into the next tax bracket, so I'm going to take home less!" That's not how it works. The tax system is a progressive tax, and so the more income you earn, the more the rate of tax you pay increases. But still, the more you make, the more you take home. It's just that each additional dollar is taxed at a higher percentage, but the first dollars are still taxed the same. Repeated, moving into a higher tax bracket affects the last of your dollars you earn, but the first dollars are still taxed at the same rate. Remember, it is always in your best interest to make more money!

The above is called your "marginal tax bracket" or "tax rate," and knowing that can help you better plan to reduce your taxes. You can look up what your tax rate is at www.irs.gov or in the charts at the end of this chapter. Your tax bracket is the tax on each additional dollar you earn in wages or investments, and you should notice there are only six federal income tax rates. So, for example, if you earn 4 percent interest on a savings account and you are in a 28 percent tax bracket, the net "after-tax" interest you earn is actually 28 percent less or 2.88 percent (4 percent x [1 − 0.28]). If the investment was a "tax-free" municipal bond paying 4 percent interest instead, you earn a real net 4 percent, since there is no federal tax on municipal bond interest. The above shows that avoiding taxes (tax-free) or even delaying them (tax-deferred) allows you to keep more of what you earn so your wealth can grow quicker.

Taxes also can be saved if you take advantage of "deductions" that reduce your taxable income. For example, if you defer $5,000 this year into a 401(k)—since 401(k) deferrals reduce your taxable wages—it will save you $1,400 in federal taxes ($5,000 x 28 percent). Generally, the same tax savings is afforded to you for other tax deductions like gifts to charities, home mortgage interest, and property taxes. Developing a relationship with a qualified tax accountant or certified public accountant can be very profitable, as they can help you take advantage of the tax deductions you qualify for. More details on tax-advantaged investing are described in Chapter 7.

Implement a "wish list" to tackle large purchases.

Another problem that prevents model budgets from balancing in reality is a lack of planning for larger expenses. These might include a big vacation, major home repairs, or furniture purchases. By not planning how you will pay for them in advance, they generally become debt (and stress) that costs you interest. Worse yet, the credit card payments spent to pay off the item could have been invested and cost you the opportunity to earn interest, dividends or investment gains that build wealth.

A simple strategy for more easily addressing major expenses is to develop a wish list of all the things you want and need to spend money on in the next several years. Try to anticipate, be honest with yourself about what you need and want, and define the dollar cost of each. Then reprioritize the list from most to least important. Do this by asking yourself, "Do I really need this item, or is it simply a desire—something I could live without?" Needs obviously take priority over desires. Finally, determine the time frame in which you would like to make each purchase.

For most lawyers, when you total all the expenses on the wish list, it should be obvious that to get everything you want costs a lot more money than you have today. So, the best approach is to look at your top priorities and determine how many months it would take you to accumulate the money needed to address them. You should save or escrow each month for these items over time into a separate "working capital" bank savings or money market mutual fund account. For example, if you need new car tires in six months that will cost you $600, set aside $100 per month for the next six months.

The wish list is an interactive, constantly changing list you should always be working on. We have seen that if you can simply list your **subjective** potential purchases, you will become more **objective** and less compulsive in your decisions about what to buy. You may also find yourself removing items from the list after thinking through whether you really need or want them, which will help you to better apply your money to your true priorities. See the "Wish List" Worksheet at the end of this chapter to help you develop your own system.

Plan for surprises with an "emergency/opportunity fund."

One of the most common destroyers of budgets is the all-too-common "emergency" expense. No matter how much you try to plan ahead, emergency expenses still occur. They may be unexpected car repairs or unanticipated medical bills. There are also financial opportunities that seem to come just when you cannot afford to take advantage of them.

The method of addressing unexpected financial needs is to establish an emergency/opportunity fund. This is another bank savings or money market account you can quickly access without penalty, because you never know when you will need the cash for the emergency or opportunity. The more cash you have built up, the more you are able to "self-insure" for uncertainties, and the higher deductibles you can carry on your insurance policies will save you on premiums. Also, when you have an opportunity, you can take advantage of it by "borrowing from yourself" using the cash in this account and "paying yourself back" later. This is far less costly than the interest cost of borrowing from a bank or credit card.

How much you should have built up is a personal calculation and is not as simple as the "three to six months income" mantra you often hear. You need to determine the amount you need for emergencies based on your own situation. Most lawyers have far too little saved in cash accounts because they assume nothing will ever happen to them. Then when one or two unexpected expenses occur, they are forced to sell valuable growth assets, draining the size of their financial house. There is little wonder why wealth never accumulates.

Start with enough to cover your auto and homeowner's deductibles. Then, look at where your income comes from—if your job is unstable or you want to make a job change, you may need several months of expenses saved up to live on if you become unemployed. If you are in solo practice or in a small law firm partnership, you will want to keep several months expenses around so you can draw yourself a salary, especially during the leaner income months. Then look at "what could break down that you have to fix." If your car is older and requiring more frequent repairs, you will need more cash set aside for that than someone who has a new car, and so on.

Save and invest within time frames.

How should you go about saving and investing? Do it allocating percentages of your total saving/investing each month (the total in Section B of your model budget) first by time frame—short term, medium term, and long term. Short term is defined as addressing things from today until the next two years. Since you may use this money in a relatively short period of time, you must also keep it liquid (easily turned into cash). You also cannot afford to lose it, so you do not put it at risk. You save, not invest, for short-term goals, which is why bank savings accounts, money market accounts, bank certificates, U.S. savings bonds, or money market mutual funds are used for short-term savings.

Investing is when you take risk—facing possible loss of principal—with the hope for earning higher-potential long-term returns. This risk or volatility can affect you less if you have a longer-term time frame until you need the money. You should only invest money you can afford to lose. So for medium-term goals, defined as from two years from now until age fifty-nine and a half, investment growth accumulation vehicles are used. The long-term time frame is for goals after age fifty-nine and a half—mainly for retirement—and also warrants using accumulation investments. Although fifty-nine and a half may seem like an odd age to use, it is the age after which the tax law allows you to access most retirement-type accounts without income tax penalties. A detailed discussion of these accumulation vehicles and their characteristics are outlined in the next chapter.

One caveat we must give here is not to consider investments as your emergency/opportunity fund since they fluctuate and could lose principal when and if you are forced to sell them. Although these conservative emergency fund savings-type accounts have little growth potential, they act as a critical form of "insurance," protecting against your having to deplete any of your other wealth accumulation assets.

Start now to make savings and investing a habit.

We cannot emphasize enough the importance of starting saving and investing as early in your career as possible so it gets ingrained as a habit. Regular saving and investing are the basic raw materials that build wealth. Even if you start out small, you need to use the big advantages you have of time and compounding.

To understand the importance of starting early, let's compare two investors. Mary invests $2,000 a year at 9 percent (monthly compounding) starting right out of law school at age twenty-five, then invests nothing after age thirty-five. Bill waits until he is 35 to invest the same $2,000 a year and contributes every year through age sixty-five. Now Mary and Bill are both ready to retire. Mary contributed $22,000 over ten years and accumulated $550,371. Bill socked away $62,000 over thirty years and accumulated only $335,831. Mary invested less yet her nest egg is over $214,540 larger than Bill's! Bill never catches up!

Your investments may do better or worse, and this is only illustrative, but understand that it really costs you if you wait to get started. The following chart illustrates the monthly savings amount required to accumulate $1,000,000 at age sixty-five assuming 10 and 8 percent annual rates of return:

The Cost of Waiting to Invest

Age	Monthly Savings Amount @ 10%	@ 8%
25	$158	$287
35	$492	$671
45	$1316	$1698
55	$4882	$5467

To further stress the importance of saving at an early age, the following chart illustrates, at 9 percent interest, the amount of money a person would have in a tax-deferred retirement plan at age sixty-five **if** they started saving $10,000 per year at various ages:

Age to Start Saving $10,000 Per Year	Account Balance at Age 65
25	$3,682,918
35	$1,485,752
45	$557,645
55	$165,602

All of these examples illustrate the power of compound interest. Even small amounts early in life can have a huge impact in your retirement account balances.

How Much Should I Be Saving?

First, you have to save something each month no matter how small. Start with the basic amount of 1 percent of your gross income. Your goal should be to work up to saving and investing around 20 percent of your gross income each year, because most retirement projections show that if you do not, you will run out of money long before your life expectancy. This is especially true if social security makes more cuts and law firms continue to cut back on their pension plan benefits. If you are getting a later start in your mid-thirties, you may need to be saving even more. Some years you will save less, and others more, just so you can hit the 20 percent average over your working years. Most people who are wealthy do this habitually as outlined in the book, *The Millionaire Next Door*, by Thomas Stanley and William Danko. This book is a must-read for young lawyers, as it lays out clear research that shows how people become multimillionaires and why so many lawyers do not.

Essential Disciplines for Wealth-Building

The more lawyers we coach, we find they need less financial planning advice and more personal financial discipline to achieve their goals. These are some self-imposed practices we find work the best to build wealth regularly from your income:

1. Automate your savings and investing. Treat your investment amount as a bill you pay out every month. If you don't get in the habit of saving money on a regular basis either through a payroll deduction or an automatic withdrawal from your checking account, the money you intended to go toward savings or investments is simply spent elsewhere. Initially, it is not the amount being saved that is important, but the habit being formed.

2. Every year, gradually increase the amount you save and invest. This strategy really accelerates the compounding of wealth.

3. You need to save and invest for all time frames at once. You can save most of your money on one time frame like the short term—building up your emergency savings account—but still should be investing smaller amounts in mutual funds for medium-term goals and through your 401(k) for retirement in the long term. You cannot afford to miss the advantages and returns that arise from diverse accumulation vehicles.

4. Do not decrease the amount you are saving and investing each month. Try not to go backward. It is amazing how easily you can redefine the purpose for what you originally set out to save and invest for, and just use the money to buy "things" instead. Lawyers also have the propensity to sell investments well before they have ever grown to the potential they could have.

5. Be careful not to adjust your lifestyle spending to your higher income when you get raises and bonuses. Always living below your means is a great

defense for surviving if your income ever decreases. It also avoids having to sell assets to live on, which results in lost future wealth growth and undermines your financial security. Lawyers need to identify an average, or base income level and budget, to spend at and not go above it. They need to know the minimum they need to earn to pay the bills and have a pre-thought-out plan for what to do with the excess income when they make more.

6. The lower the percentage of your net worth is attributable to cars and your personal residence, the higher the probability you are on your way to meeting your accumulation goals. Large houses (large mortgage debt) and expensive cars (a depreciating asset) drain wealth, because they decrease your ability to save and invest elsewhere. Buy a smaller house than the bank says you can afford, and look at buying lower-priced used cars and running them longer.

7. Live mostly a cash lifestyle—pay as you go! You may realize that after a few months you do not need some of the things you have been wasting your money on. Simple living can reap contentment and more cash to save and invest. Vow to go back to the days of cash-only transactions for everything other than your large monthly payments, and even those if you want to get really serious. Stop using your debit and credit cards or writing checks for day-to-day expenditures like groceries, drugstore items, clothing, and so on. It feels much different when you have to shell out $50 cash for a purchase than handing over a piece of plastic.

Debt Reduce and Save and Invest

We find the majority of today's young lawyers are carrying a large amount of debt that consists of mainly college loans and even car loans, personal loans, and credit card debts. Most start out with their financial house "under water," because these debts are far greater than their assets. We are often asked about the best strategies for paying off those debts as fast as possible first, as if it was the only goal they ever wanted to achieve.

Our first strategy is to tell young lawyers they cannot afford to focus on **only one** financial goal—no matter what it is—when they really have many issues they want and need to address in their lifetimes. Imagine scraping together every last dollar you can save each month to pay off your debts at the cost of having no emergency funds. Then, when your next emergency expense arrives, you have no choice but to use the credit card to pay for it, resulting in being back in the same debt again! Or the cost of not securing insurance coverages early on results in permanently higher insurance premiums the rest of your life.

A solid financial plan addresses multiple concerns simultaneously, not just the first one, then once completed, moves you on to the next, and so on. This "sequential" type focus results in the loss of valuable time needed to get invested money compounding faster and to quickly develop critical financial habits discussed throughout this chapter. So you have to be working on addressing all parts of your financial plan and all of your goals at the same time (concurrently). Although you may have significant debts, you cannot be defined and overwhelmed by them. They will be paid off someday, and your plan will address them, but it is more critical to be more savings- and investment-focused to develop wealth over the long run. The "cost of waiting" chart presented earlier shows how costly it is to put off starting to invest now.

So, the first strategy is to save and invest and reduce debt at the same time. Can you imagine using all your monthly savings paying off your debts for five years and missing the 3 percent match (free money) compounding and growing in the 401(k) you avoided starting? If your debts are the largest priority, then just put the greatest percentage of what you can save each month toward paying them off. But you still must save and invest in other areas, even if the amounts are small. You need to reinforce the positive habit of saving at the same time you are paying off the past. Yes, this method may cost you some loan interest, but it will cost you even more if you never learn to save. We find that if you do not start addressing short-, medium-, and long-term saving and investing together right away, the chances that you will never address those areas significantly go up. Procrastination and excuses creep in and before you know it, you have lost the time and compounding necessary to achieve the goal. The main reason lawyers do not reach their financial goals is because they don't have enough assets built up to address them, not because all their debts are paid off.

For student loans, realize that you can consolidate and/or combine them into one loan at a fixed rate by July first every year. Once you have consolidated, your interest rate will be locked for the next thirty years if your balance exceeds $60,000. The longer the loan period, the lower the minimum payment and the less pressure on your cash flow. Most consolidation programs offer further rate reductions for automating your payment and for successive on-time payments. The interest rate charged on new and non-consolidated federal student loans changes each year on July first.

Rates will most likely rise in the future for new federal loans and non-consolidated loans. Deciding whether to consolidate as rates climb could be a difficult decision. You can only consolidate your loans one time. If you consolidated your loans in the late 1990s, you locked in a much higher rate than today's. Unfortunately, you cannot reconsolidate to take advantage of lower rates available now, so you may have to consider paying extra on higher-rate student loans.

You can make additional payments on your student loans without penalty to accelerate your debt reduction goals. So the main motivation to reduce, for example, a 3 percent student loan, is only the good feeling of moving toward becoming debt-free. Your net worth, however, can grow faster by paying off higher-interest debt and/or investing at an after-tax rate of greater than 3 percent. You just need to compare the interest rate cost of student loans versus other debts and what you could earn from investing to see the best debts to pay back or if investing makes more sense.

If you have personal debts like credit cards or high-interest personal loans, these are a higher priority to pay off than most student loans, especially if their interest rates are above 10 percent. Prioritize your debts based on interest rates, and eliminate the loans starting from the highest to the lowest rate. However, you may want to "kick start" your debt reduction process by paying off some of the smaller loan amounts if you can first, especially those that have higher minimum payment requirements than others. That way, your cash flow is freed up by the higher payment, and you can use it to further accelerate your other saving, investing, and debt reduction goals.

Once you pay off higher-cost consumer debts like credit cards, cut them up. Have one or two credit cards at the most to simplify your life and to reduce the chance you will overspend again. The bottom line is that whatever caused the consumer debt to build up should not be repeated. You need to follow a budget system to live within your means and not "bail yourself out" by using credit cards to finance your budgeting imbalance rather than dealing with getting your spending under control. Not everything you buy is a need. You face many more "desires" every day that you can live without, and you need to learn to control them or say "No." Just say "No" for a while as you pay debts off, and you will see a more rapid reduction in the debt pressure you have.

You can also shift higher-interest credit card balances to lower-interest ones, but remember that does not get them paid off sooner. If you have equity built up in your home, you can also take out a home equity loan or line and pay off your high-cost consumer debts. The home equity or line is income tax-deductible interest and may provide you with a lower payment, but you still need to compare interest rates, payoff periods, monthly payment amounts, and other personal factors to see if this type of consolidation makes sense.

With mortgage and business debt, a similar analysis should be applied as to whether you should pay them off earlier. However, mortgage and business debt have the additional advantage of being income tax-deductible. Student loans are only tax-deductible if you make less than $60,000 as a single taxpayer and $100,000 if you are married. The interest rate to use is the after-tax rate. For instance, a 6 percent mortgage, for someone in a 33 percent tax bracket, has an after-tax rate cost of only 4.02 percent (6 percent x [1 − 0.33]).

When purchasing a home, one rule you may want to follow is to try not to finance more than two and a half times your annual income if you want to be financially independent at an earlier age. It is also advantageous to minimize the number of personal residence transactions you engage in, because they involve substantial fees, commissions, and transaction costs. You should also avoid private mortgage, if possible, which is generally applied to mortgages that are greater than 80 percent of a home's purchase price. You can do this by making a down payment of 20 percent or more of the homes purchase price or through a combination of two loans. One loan is a traditional mortgage, and the other is held by a bank as a home equity loan or line of credit.

Also consider how long you plan on staying in a home when determining the best financing. If you plan to be in a home for only five years, you should consider an adjustable rate mortgage (ARM) like a 5/1 ARM versus a fixed thirty-year loan. The interest rate will be lower on the 5/1 ARM, since the lender is only guaranteeing your rate for five as opposed to thirty years, even though both loans are amortized over thirty years. Remember too, a shorter-term fifteen-year fixed rate loan has a much higher minimum payment, which will cost you your ability to save and invest. For a more detailed discussion of how much of a home you can "afford," see the discussion on real estate in Chapter 6.

Finally, it is a good idea to review your credit report every year. The financial information included in this report will have a bearing on whether you can obtain a loan, auto or home insurance, rent an apartment, or even apply for a job. Go to the central Web site at www.annualcreditreport.com to request a free credit file disclosure report once every twelve months from each of the three nationwide credit reporting companies. Contact these credit bureaus if you find any errors so they can be corrected.

Maximize Your Bonus or Large Case Fee

Another common budgeting question lawyers ask us is how to best manage the receipt of larger lump sums of money. The money could be from a bonus, a large case fee, or even an inheritance. As we emphasized before, you cannot focus on one goal with money to get the most out of it to build your financial house. So when you receive this cash, realize that you only have four major things you can do with the money: spend it, invest it, reduce debt, and/or save it. The acronym to remind you of the decision-making framework is SIRS.

SIRS is a powerful decision-making tool, because it provides a fixed template to test any action you contemplate with regard to using money.

Here are some questions to ask to help you compare the opportunity cost and benefits of adding more or less money to each of these four categories when dividing it up:

- SPEND: Do I have a need on my wish list that I must address?
- INVEST: Have I added to my accumulation goals enough this year?
- REDUCE DEBT: Are there any high-interest debts I can pay off or down to get a certain return?
- SAVE: Is my emergency/opportunity fund cash at an adequate level?

Since you cannot predict the future to know whether one of these areas would turn out better than the other, it is often prudent to put money toward all four areas with the larger percentage to areas that address your financial priorities. Since you may have several goals with your money, this approach of addressing all four areas is generally a prudent approach.

"Savings to Spend" Account Expense* Worksheet

(Listed chronologically in the order they are due)

Irregular Expense	Annual Cost	Monthly Cost	Date(s) Due	Date Paid
Examples:				
Water/Sewer Bill	$240	$20	4/1	
Anniversary Present	$300	$25	5/3	
Annual Vacation	$1500	$125	8/1	
Christmas Gifts	$1200	$100	12/31	

Total Annual Cost $3240

Total Monthly Cost $270

(Annual cost divided by 12)

(The above monthly cost should be escrowed/saved into your savings to spend account each month.)

Basic Federal Tax Estimator

(This is a guide only. This does not factor in credits, phase-outs, child care, student loan interest deductions, moving expenses, etc.)

Income

Wages and Salaries	$_____
Taxable Interest and Dividends	$_____
Business Income (Loss)	$_____
Capital Gains (Loss)	$_____
Rental Income, Partnerships, S Corporations, Trusts	$_____
Other Income:	$_____

Total Income: $_____

Less: Adjustments to Income

IRA Deduction	$_____
Self-Employed SEP, SIMPLE IRA	$_____
Other:	$_____

Total Adjustments   ($_____)

Total Adjusted Gross Income (AGI)
(Total Income Less Total Adjustments) $_____

Less: The Higher of Itemized Deductions OR Your Standard Deduction   ($_____)

Standard Deduction 2006   Single $5,150
Standard Deduction 2006   Married $10,300

OR

Itemized Deductions:

Medical and Dental Expenses	$_____
(only amounts greater than 7.5% of AGI)	
State and Local Taxes	$_____
Property Taxes	$_____
Home Mortgage Interest	$_____
Gifts to Charity	$_____
Misc. Deductions	$_____
(only amounts greater than 2% of AGI)	

Total Itemized Deductions $_____

Less: Personal Exemptions: ($_____)
2006: $3,300 Times # in Your Household

Equals Taxable Income: $_____
Federal Tax Due (From Tables Below) $_____

Monthly Federal Taxes:
  Federal Taxes Above Divided by 12: $_____
Per Paycheck Federal Taxes:
  Federal Taxes Above Divided by # Paychecks in a Year
                                                    $_____

Marginal Tax Rate: *See Table Below*   _____%

SINGLE Filing Chart		
2006 Federal Income Tax Rates		
If taxable income is over	**But not over**	**The tax is:**
$0	$7,550	10% of the amount over $0
$7,550	$30,650	$755 plus 15% of the amount over $7,550
$30,650	$74,200	$4,220 plus 25% of the amount over $30,650
$74,200	$154,800	$15,108 plus 28% of the amount over $74,200
$154,800	$336,550	$37,676 plus 33% of the amount over 154,800
$336,500	No limit	$97,653 plus 35% of the amount over 336,550
MARRIED Filing Jointly Chart		
2006 Federal Income Tax Rates		
If taxable income is over	**But not over**	**The tax is:**
$0	$15,100	10% of the amount over $0
$15,100	$61,300	$1,510 plus 15% of the amount over $15,100
$61,300	$123,700	$8,440 plus 25% of the amount over $61,300
$123,700	$188,450	$24,040 plus 28% of the amount over $123,700
$188,450	$336,550	$42,170 plus 33% of the amount over $188,450
$336,500	No limit	$91,043 plus 35% of the amount over 336,550

"Wish List" Worksheet for Larger Purchases
(Listed by Priority)

Last Time Reviewed/Updated: _____

Item to Purchase	Total Cost	Time Frame Desired	Need (N) or Desire(D)?	Priority
Examples:				
New Car tires	$600	6 months	N	1
New Winter Coat	$500	8 months	N	2
Upgrade Wardrobe	$1200	12 months	N	3
Piano	$5000	3 years	D	
New Furniture	$5000	4 years	D	
New Used Car	$25000	5 years	D	
Europe Vacation	$6000	7 years	D	

Total Cost of "Wish List" Purchases: **$43,300**

6

The Growth Accumulation Level

This level represents an overall goal to develop the largest amount of assets—the largest financial house—you can build over your lifetime. Almost all the investment choices are quite varied in their features, benefits, risks, and potential returns. Some of these investments may include individual stocks and bonds, mutual funds, variable life insurance cash values, annuities, college savings programs, IRAs, employer-sponsored retirement plans such as 401(k)s and pension plans, real estate equity, or your practice value. The majority of your financial independence will come from these investments. While some of these assets are liquid and can serve as part of emergency reserves, their investment horizon is usually five years or longer and perform best when they are left to grow.

A Discussion of Risk

Keep in mind that all investments have risk. There is no such thing as a risk-free investment. However, there are varying degrees and types of risk. The risk most often associated with an investment involves fluctuation or loss of principal (the amount you invested) like a sudden depreciation in the stock market, as in October of 1987, or a bear market (a period of downturn in the stock market) as in 2000 to 2002. Here are some of the other forms of risk besides market risk:

Purchasing power risk: Another term for this is "inflation." If the cost for products and services rises faster than the interest rate being credited on your savings and checking accounts, you are exposed to purchasing power risk. While you don't lose any principal, you are still losing ground relative to inflation. Your dollars may not be able to buy as much as when you originally invested. This is a particular problem currently for retirees who have traditionally held bank CDs and lived off the interest each year.

Interest rate risk: Bonds and fixed income securities are subject to this risk. Your principal value can decline if interest rates climb quickly. The severity of the loss is often magnified by the duration and/or maturity of the bonds and the credit quality. At this time, when interest rates are near historical lows, many people who own fixed income securities are unknowingly subjecting their investments to interest rate risk.

Business risk: This is the risk of losing money due to circumstances out of your control. A business could go bankrupt and your investment becomes worthless due to the market for the companies product drying up, or because of a lawsuit tying up the companies time and resources.

Liquidity risk: This is the risk associated with being invested in real estate, limited partnerships, businesses, and other investments where there is sometimes no immediate market for your investment. This is problematic if you have a need for cash and you cannot sell or liquidate your shares. You would invest in something like this only if you had sufficient assets available besides this investment.

Regulatory risk: Investors run the risk that government policy decisions or influences of society as a whole could endanger an investment's value. Environmental and tax legislation can have a dramatic impact on certain investment values, up or down. It is important to note this risk when investing.

Currency risk: An investment in international securities can be affected by foreign exchange rate changes, political and economic instability, as well as differences in accounting standards.

Diversity risk: This will be discussed at length later in this chapter, but allow us to overstate the obvious: DIVERSIFY!

A final "risk" we see our clients face is the tendency to consume too much and to prematurely liquidate investments that have been established subverting their long term growth potential. To reduce this "consumption risk", you must live below your total income, and develop a self imposed rule not to touch what you have set aside for long term accumulation until retirement. Keeping up with the Jones has become a national epidemic—especially lawyers who seem ever compelled to "look the part." But the real truth is that the millionaires who live next door don't concern themselves with flaunting their wealth, which explains one important reason why they are wealthy.

In summary, a properly structured financial plan will balance all of these variables so you are diversified by asset class, risk levels, tax treatment, and time horizon.

Real Estate

For many lawyers, one of their most substantial assets can be their personal residence or home. Generally speaking, real estate has long been considered an "investment" tool for its favorable tax benefits and its historical appreciation. Although there can be significant investment benefits in the long term, buying and owning real estate is not without risks. Deflation may decrease property values, or expected long-term growth in a given area may not occur. Changes in tax law may reduce or eliminate anticipated tax benefits. Also, real estate is not liquid, so the necessity of a quick sale may force a substantial reduction in its sale price.

We have found it prudent to have lawyers treat their personal residence or home as an expense, not as an investment. This focus will actually help you to spend less for your home rather than overspending for it. In general, buy a home you can afford, which we define as one whose mortgage payment, property taxes, and ongoing repair costs still allow you to save and invest enough to reach your overall financial goals. Overspending, whether it's for a home or any item, always takes away from your ability to save and invest for other more important goals like college and retirement. Overspending on a home is too often justified by telling (i.e., kidding) ourselves that our home is an "investment." Investing in other vehicles could generate higher returns than your home, so the key is to be diversified. You do not want to be "house poor," which means your only "asset" is your home, which the bank owns most of anyway. In Texas, they would call you "Big Hat, No Cattle" (i.e., big house, no other real wealth).

If your home grows phenomenally in value, great. The easiest financial issue to face is where to put excess money. But if it does not grow that much, your overall financial plan still must work. It is a false sense of comfort thinking your home's growth will bail you out of not saving and investing enough. Homes have been the darlings of the decade so far. Housing prices could decline or continue increasing. Either way, the "wealth effect" caused by your increasing home value should not lull you into ignoring other important investment strategies.

We don't see too many lawyers selling their homes when they retire, buying a much cheaper double-wide trailer to live in, and then investing the difference with us. They love their homes—they are places of great comfort and emotional value, and they stay in them. Another problem with counting on homes as a retirement asset is you cannot rent them out or tear off a wall and sell that part to get retirement income. Yes, you can borrow against a home, but that is still building debt that **costs** you money, not wealth that **earns** you money. Even if they do sell their home, they end up spending more than what they sold it for on the retirement condo in Florida!

A popular question we get from many young lawyers is, "Should I buy a home right away out of law school?" In general, jumping into any large investment or large expense area, homes included, without a financial foundation of insurance and secure cash flow management is not sound. When you have just started your first job, you need several months of income and living at least to determine your model budget (see Chapter 2), so renting is best starting out. You are not always "throwing money down the drain" with renting. You are buying cash flow freedom from large mortgage payments, property taxes, repair costs, and home maintenance, just to name a few. You also have the flexibility to move anytime. You also can afford to invest more if your cash flow is not swallowed up by the costs of owning a home. Investing in other vehicles could also generate higher returns and build your financial house for you quicker. Besides, you won't rent forever. Buying a home does offer solid long-term financial and non-financial security you will want to take advantage of eventually.

There are also many other non-financial issues that should be resolved since they impact whether you should buy or rent. After you are more settled in your job and area, for example, you may want to buy a home. But be careful, as young lawyers change jobs frequently, forcing them to sell that home too quickly and be forced to take a loss. The home you buy should be at the price where the mortgage payments, property taxes, insurance, and regular repairs each month still allow you to save and invest enough to reach your goals. We call this your "personal home affordability index." The additional cost of owning a home above your current rent situation, even after tax deductions, will always reduce your monthly saving, investing, and debt reducing capacity. It is prudent in the beginning stage of your law career to value building saving, investment, and reducing debt as primary habits more than getting into mortgage debt to own a home. If you can buy a home whose payment and repairs (after tax deductions) is the same as your current rent cost, only then should you consider buying.

Investing in real estate such as a duplex or rental apartments faces the same risks noted above for personal residences as well as the added risks of higher-than-expected repair and improvement costs. Also, rents may not cover the property's mortgage and other expenses, not to mention tenant problems. A discussion of the pros and cons of whether you should buy investment real estate is beyond the scope of this book. However, we find there are numerous non-financial (i.e., do you really have time and skills to manage rental property?) as well as financial (i.e., real estate can grow in value and provide you with positive cash flow) aspects that must be considered.

Stocks

The terms "stock" and "share" refer to a partial ownership or equity interest in a corporation. As a stockholder, you'll be able to vote for the company's board of directors and receive information on the firm's activities and business results. You may share in "dividends" or current profits.

Investors typically buy and hold stocks for their long-term growth potential. Stocks with a history of regular dividends are often held for both income and growth. As the long-term growth of a company cannot be predicted, the short-term market value of the company's stock will fluctuate. If your financial need or your fear cause you to sell when the market (and your stock's price) is "down" (also called a "bear market"), a capital loss can result. If the market is "up" (also called a "bull market"), an investor could then realize a capital gain if the stock is sold.

Bonds

While stocks represent ownership in a business, bonds are debt issued by institutions such as the federal government, corporations, and state and local governments. At the bonds' "maturity," the principal amount will be returned. In the meantime, bondholders receive interest. When first issued, a bond will have a specified interest rate, or "yield." If a bond is traded (bought or sold) on a public exchange, the market price or value will fluctuate, generally with changes in interest rates. Bonds are most often used to receive a stable source of current income.

Mutual Funds

Using a mutual fund is an excellent way to lower your investment risk, because they are diversified from owning a number of stocks and bonds. A properly designed mutual fund portfolio (i.e., several types of funds) is generally the most appropriate method of accumulating wealth at this level in your financial house. Some funds have high "market risk," meaning they can fluctuate quite dramatically. Past experience shows that funds with the most risk have upside and downside potential that needs to be carefully considered. Funds with low market risk often have "inflation risk." These funds usually produce lower returns that may not keep up with inflation.

If your investment horizon is relatively short (up to five years), a more conservatively balanced fund, equity income fund, or even a short- to medium-term corporate bond or government bond fund may be the most appropriate. When your investment horizon is longer, growth-oriented stock funds are generally going to be the better choice. Again, each investor's circumstance is different, and the advice of a competent professional will be valuable. Most firms have a short investment risk attitude questionnaire you can complete to help you determine your risk nature and the appropriate portfolio strategy to meet your needs.

Dollar Cost Averaging Strategy

An additional strategy to employ when investing includes dollar cost averaging. Dollar cost averaging is the process of investing a fixed amount of money each month (or quarter, or year) without worrying about whether the market is up or down. When it is down, you will buy more shares, bringing your average share price down. Over time, besides the element of forced savings, you will hopefully see returns you are happy with. Dollar cost averaging does not assure a profit, nor does it protect against loss in declining markets. This investment strategy requires regular investments regardless of the fluctuating price of the investment. You should consider your financial ability to continue investing through periods of low price levels. An application of this strategy would be to electronically invest $250 per month, from your checking account, on the fifteenth of each month, into a mutual fund.

Portfolio Rebalancing Strategy

When there is a large amount of money to invest, coming up with an investment policy or model allocation and adhering to it is a must. Once an overall asset allocation model is chosen based on your goals and risk nature, stick to it and change only if there are significant changes in the economy, the portfolio, and/or your goals and objectives. Then, on a regular basis (either quarterly, semiannually, or annually) rebalance the portfolio back to the asset allocation you started with. With this strategy, your investment mix does not get skewed towards more or less risk and volatility.

Many portfolio managers and investment programs now can provide this rebalancing process on an automatic basis. A practical application of this is in managing your 401(k) retirement plan (defined in Chapter 7). Set percentages of how much to invest in each of the plan investment options in which you want to invest. Then, at least once per year, reset the dollar amounts (or percentages) in each option so they are at the correct percentages you started with.

Diversification is Key

Diversify! Diversify! Diversify! Nothing else will be as crucial to your portfolio as diversifying and having a long-term vision. It's important to diversity not only by asset class, but also by tax treatment and time horizon. You know the proverb, "Don't put all your eggs in one basket." Well, take it to the extreme: Don't put all the baskets on the same truck, and don't drive all the trucks down the same road! It's not necessary to look too far back to recall the faddish investing in technology and startup companies of the late 1990s. Many investors lost too much when these overvalued stocks plunged, and eager investors expecting big returns were left with substantial losses.

Sometimes misunderstood, the main goal of diversification is not to maximize your return, but to minimize your risk and lower your volatility. You also need to stay with your diversification plan. A basic underlying premise is that there is as much risk in being out of the stock market when it goes up as being in the stock market when it goes down, especially for your long-term money. As an example, look at the growth of $10,000 invested over the ten-year period ending December 31, 2004. Using the unmanaged S&P 500 stock index, you would have experienced the following results*:

Stayed Fully Invested (2,530 days)	$26,388
Missed Ten Best Months	$16,451
Missed Twenty Best Months	$11,335
Missed Thirty Best Months	$8,134

Results based on S&P composite index with dividends taken in cash. The S&P 500 is an unmanaged group of stocks representative of the stock market in general. You cannot invest directly in an index. Past performance does not guarantee future returns. Investment will fluctuate and, when redeemed, may be worth more or less than originally purchased.

So, if you were out of the market during the ten, twenty, or even the thirty top-performing months, you would have ended up with significantly lower returns. It is **time in** the stock market (holding for the long term) **not timing** the market (frequent short-term buying and selling) that helps you make more money. While diversification does not guarantee against loss, it is an important method used to manage risk.

One example of how to diversify a portfolio is outlined by the following decisions:

- Stocks versus bonds versus cash (asset class)
- U.S. (domestic) versus international securities (country)*
- Large cap versus small cap stocks (company size)**
- Growth versus value stocks (style)
- Bond quality (high, medium, low risk)
- Bond length (short, medium, long)

Investment risks associated with international investing, in addition to other risks, include currency fluctuations, political and economic instability, and differences in accounting standards.
** *Investments in smaller company and micro-cap stocks generally carry a higher level of volatility and risk over the short term.*

We have learned that there is no consistent pattern that can predict when and if one asset class or style will over- or under-perform. So, investing is not as much about **predicting** the market's future moves but much more about **positioning** your money currently across various asset classes and styles. No one asset class stays on top or at the bottom for too long. They also do not all move in the same direction at the same time.

There are many good resources to turn to that will help you take this process much further than the scope of this book. We think some of the best information can come from a competent and qualified financial advisor who will listen to you and develop an investment plan that meets your needs and risk nature.

In general, a higher investment risk is best for those who:

- Can accept short-term losses
- Can buy shares during a down market
- Believe gains will offset losses over the long run

- Will not leave the investment if one or two bad years occur
- Have a long investment time horizon

The best way to learn sound market advice is to listen to the experts. The following quotes from these mutual fund leaders all stress the futility of market timing:

Peter Lynch: *"My single-most important piece of investment advice is to ignore the short-term fluctuations of the market. From one year to the next, the stock market is a coin flip. It can go up or down. The real money in stocks is made in the third, fourth, and fifth year of your investments, because you are participating in a company's earnings, which grow over time."*

Warren Buffet: *"I do not have, never have had, and never will have an opinion where the stock market will be a year from now."*

Sir John Templeton: *"Ignore fluctuations. Do not try to outguess the stock market. Buy a quality portfolio and invest for the long term."*

So, to drive it home, invest for the long term and be patient!

7

Tax-Advantaged Accumulation

No discussion about investing would be complete without understanding an investment's tax features and benefits. Tax planning with investments in its simplicity is the avoidance, reduction, deferral, or minimization of the tax due on the growth and/or income produced by the investment. The lower the taxes on the investment's growth or income, the higher its return and the more wealth—the bigger the financial house—you can build up. The more you can put off or delay paying those taxes (tax deferral), the more your investment can grow for you in the meantime.

In the previous chapter, we outlined investments that are considered to be "non-qualified" assets. The term "non-qualified" commonly refers to investment/accounts that do not meet the criteria for being a qualified plan under the IRS code. Generally, nonqualified assets are those assets which are not eligible for an immediate income tax deduction for the contribution to the account. But some non-qualified investments can offer benefits that can defer or delay payment of income taxes and even avoid them altogether by being tax-free. Some non-qualified investments can be more liquid (can be turned into cash quickly) and generally without substantial tax penalties for doing so.

Retirement accounts are often referred to as "qualified" plans since, if they are managed within their IRS-outlined tax rules, they "qualify" for sometimes more favorable tax treatments like an income tax-deductible contributions and tax-deferred growth. Upon withdrawal at retirement, for example, you may have to pay income taxes on the amount withdrawn, depending on the type of qualified plan. Essentially, you trade off the income tax deduction on the contributions now for payment of the taxes due on all of the retirement account later.

Realize that some investments have tax benefits that can make them look like both non-qualified and qualified investments. Just be clear what the investment can and cannot do for you. Also, to receive the investment's tax benefits, there are often tradeoffs or restrictions on using the investment's features as set out by IRS tax rules. For example, to avoid the tax penalties of early withdrawals (10 percent federal and often an additional state tax penalty) from an IRA and to get its maximum tax deferral, you cannot access it until age fifty-nine and a half. When the tax benefit's advantages are tied to other features in the investment, you need to consider your goals for the money invested, income tax bracket, need for liquidity, and risk nature before you invest.

Also, knowing your income tax bracket (see Chapter 5 discussion) now and during retirement is important in making investment choices. At the same time, income tax rates have and will change, and no one really can know for certain about future tax rates. This is why it is important to remain flexible in your tax and investment strategy, not relying too much on any one tax law or investment, as the tax law and its treatment of investments may change. So, diversify your investment not only by strategy, but also by tax treatment. It is also important to work with a qualified tax accountant like a certified public accountant (CPA) as part of your planning team to help you implement the best tax strategies for you.

The following outlines some important tax advantages and tax strategies of investments used in building the growth accumulation level of your financial house.

Tax Advantages of Common Non-Qualified Investments

Stocks: As stocks appreciate in value (for this discussion, we'll assume they appreciate) there is no tax due on the appreciation until the stock is sold. Along the way, if any dividends are paid, the federal tax rate (15 percent for the highest tax bracket) is lower than the ordinary income tax rate. In addition, when the stock is sold, if held for over a year, the gain is taxed at the lower 15 percent long-term capital gains rate. So, there is a benefit of tax deferral during the holding period and tax minimizing due to the gain being treated as a long-term capital gain for stocks held longer than 12 months.

Bonds: Generally, most bonds pay interest at a fixed rate every six months with the original principal being returned at a future set maturity date with no tax or gain. For corporate bonds, that interest is subject to ordinary income taxes. With municipal bonds, however, the interest is paid and received free of federal income tax. If you own bonds issued by the state you live in, the interest can also be state income tax-free. Bonds sold prior to the maturity date may result in taxable gain or loss.

Real estate: Real estate can be an excellent method of building wealth. Getting away from rent and into your first home is one obvious way. Another is leveraging the equity you have in your existing real estate into additional property. The growth is tax-deferred, and there are some favorable strategies available upon the sale and/or disposition. As for financing your house, contrary to popular belief, for some individuals it can make sense to put little money down and stretch the mortgage out (and the tax deduction) in favor of freeing up cash flow for other goals and objectives. For a comprehensive discussion of this topic, we would encourage you to pick up Doug Andrew's book, *Missed Fortune.*

Life insurance: The tax benefits of a life insurance policy are much like those of the Roth IRA, with some additional features. We outlined those in more detail in Chapter 4, but the fact that life insurance has many "living benefits" as well can make it an important wealth accumulator. As an accumulation tool, there is a cost for the insurance, so this is appropriate for someone who is younger, in good health and has a longer investment time horizon. The cash values inside the policy accumulate tax-deferred and can be accessed tax-free if structured properly through a combination of policy withdrawals and loans. It is generally best to avoid having the policy become a modified endowment contract, and working with a very knowledgeable insurance or financial professional is a must to maximize its potential to work for you.

Having a permanent life insurance policy can help you maximize your overall net worth in some other ways, too. You reduce your need for term insurance, which frees up cash. In fact, the most beneficial time to have a permanent life insurance policy in place is at retirement because of all the advantages it provides. Briefly, you can be more aggressive in using and enjoying your other assets, because life insurance essentially provides a "permission slip" to do so. Work with your financial advisor to coordinate this with your overall financial plan.

529 College Savings Plans: Another question we get frequently from lawyers trying to accumulate money is, "How do we fund our children's future college costs?" The direct answer we usually share here is to start investing "pre-birth" for this goal. So, for those of you without children, since college costs are increasing every year, what you start to invest in now can make a huge difference toward meeting this goal. If you have children, one of the most popular methods to accumulate money for college is through 529 College Savings Plans. These are mostly mutual funds sponsored by each of the fifty states that allow money invested to grow tax-deferred for college. Some states even allow a state tax deduction on the contributions. If the funds are withdrawn for "qualified" higher education expenses like tuition, room, and board, the funds can be withdrawn tax-free. These funds can even be transferred between family members. Be aware though, under current tax law, the favorable tax treatment of qualified 529 Plan distributions only extends to December 31, 2010. For a lengthier discussion, as well as a link to your state-sponsored plan, go to www.savingforcollege.com. Most importantly, make sure your own financial house is in order and that your plan is solid before aggressively putting money into your children's accounts.

Annuities: An annuity is marketed by an insurance company as an alternative to other investments. There are numerous benefits of non-qualified annuities; they grow tax-deferred, you can switch between the separate accounts inside a variable annuity without tax implications, and there are some death benefit guarantees to protect the value for your heirs. Withdrawals from annuities prior to age fifty-nine and a half are subject to a 10 percent early withdrawal penalty as well as potential deferred sales charges.

Roth IRAs: Assuming your income is low enough that you can use Roth IRAs, we highly recommend them. You do not get a current tax deduction, but under current law, all the growth (again, assuming it grows) is tax-free. Then, when you take the money out of the Roth IRA at retirement, you receive it tax-free. Roth IRAs are like paying tax on the seeds going into the ground now (contributions not tax-deductible) rather than the future harvest (growth on the account).

Growth in a Roth IRA may not be withdrawn until reaching age fifty-nine and a half and maintaining your Roth IRA for a period of five years. Withdrawals prior to this are subject to a 10 percent federal penalty for early withdrawals. Roth IRA limits are $4,000 in 2005 to 2007 and $5,000 in 2008 to 2010. In order to be eligible to make a maximum contribution to a Roth IRA, your modified adjusted gross income (AGI) needs to be less then $95,000 if you are single and $150,000 if you are married. You are able to make partial contributions if your AGI is between $95,000 and $110,000 if single and $150,000 to $160,000 if married. Roth IRAs have both elements of "qualified" investments—because of the tax rules you need to "qualify" to use them to receive the favorable tax treatment *and* "non-qualified" investments— because your investment contributions are made with after-tax dollars.

Be aware that in 2006, many law firm 401(k) plans will allow the addition of "Roth 401(k)" deposits, which may make Roths accessible for more attorneys. See below for a more detailed discussion of 401(k)s.

Tax Advantages of Common Qualified Retirement Investments

One method of delaying the tax involves investing dollars into qualified retirement plans. Generally, this means dollars invested are made on a before-tax or tax-deductible basis. While, the taxes are not eliminated, they are deferred until the funds are withdrawn. The most popular plans include traditional individual retirement accounts (IRAs), simplified employee pensions (SEPs), tax-sheltered annuities (TSAs or 403(b)s), pension and profit-sharing plans, and 401(k) plans.

The main advantage behind these plans is that the government has given you significant motivation to save money. This is because your taxable income is reduced dollar for dollar by the contribution, which will save you 20 to 45 percent of the deposit in income taxes (depending on your income tax bracket). While these accounts are good places to defer and delay the tax liability during your working years, they present some problems at retirement because of the tax due then. Remember, you aren't eliminating the tax, you are deferring it. Transferring qualified assets to heirs can also present some tax nightmares if not handled carefully.

The general principal here is to save money into these plans when you are in a higher income tax bracket and withdraw the funds at retirement when you are supposed to be in a lower tax bracket. However, if you do a good job saving in these plans, you may not be in a lower tax bracket at retirement due to the large amounts of money you will be pulling out of the plan when you retire. If you have taken care of the Protection Foundation and Cash Generation Levels of your financial house plan, you should then always contribute to the 401(k) up to where your law firm matches those funds if you plan to be at your current job long enough to be fully vested. Being fully "vested" means, if you leave the firm, the employer's matching funds are yours to take with you.

As your income increases, you should try to maximize your tax-deductible retirement plan contributions. We recommend you wait to maximize the contributions until the Protection and Cash Generation Levels of your financial house have been addressed. This is because the money deposited into these plans is normally not available until you reach the age of fifty-nine and a half. While there are some permitted exceptions for getting your money out early by borrowing the funds, if you are disabled, or if you have a hardship situation; for the most part, money flowing into these plans should be viewed as retirement money that cannot be touched until age fifty-nine and a half. There are income taxes and penalties for early withdrawals that will cause unnecessary outflows of cash, reducing the size of your financial house.

If you are looking for ways to reduce your taxable income, the largest tax deductions can come from qualified plans set up through your practice. A qualified plan will be appropriate if you want to reduce taxes, save for retirement, and/or reward and retain good employees. In most states, qualified plan assets are also protected from creditors.

Keep in mind that there are some drawbacks of qualified retirement plans. The money is generally not available without penalty until age fifty-nine and a half, all distributions are taxed as ordinary income when received, they often have setup and annual administration fees, and upon death, the income and estate tax consequences can be substantial if proceeds are paid to a beneficiary that is someone other than your spouse or a charity.

Here is a brief discussion of the more popular retirement plans:

Traditional deductible IRAs: You can invest up to $4,000 (2005 to 2007) for yourself in an IRA and deduct the contribution as long as you do not have another qualified plan or make a Roth IRA contribution.

If you are a solo or small firm practitioner, these are a great way to invest for retirement if you do not want to also fund a retirement plan for your staff since 100 percent of it goes directly to your IRA account. You may also be able to contribute another $4000 to an IRA for your spouse.

ROTH IRAs: These are discussed in more detail on pages 81-84 however, if you qualify, ROTH IRAs are another good option to invest for retirement as all the funding goes towards your own ROTH account and not staff. You also may qualify to fund another ROTH IRA for your spouse. Although ROTH IRAs contributions offer no income tax deduction, under current tax law you can take money out of them tax free at retirement. They also do not require you to take money out at older ages allowing them to accumulate even more for you over the long term.

SIMPLE IRAs: A SIMPLE IRA is often the starting point for a small practice. The setup and maintenance fees are minimal. A SIMPLE IRA allows for any owner or employee to contribute up to $10,000 in 2006, pre-tax, as long as $10,000 does not exceed 100 percent of income. The employer must also choose a matching contribution of 1 to 3 percent per year or a flat 2 percent contribution for any eligible employees. For example, if the practice chose a 3 percent match and a paralegal making $30,000 contributes 3 percent of his or her income to the plan, the practice would need to contribute 3 percent as well, or $900. The practice must also make a matching contribution to the owner(s)/partner(s) as well. The match is immediately vested. Vesting refers to a schedule that can be placed on certain retirement plans that requires employees to work for a specified period of time before the money contributed to the plan by the employer is theirs if they leave.

Profit-sharing plans: Profit-sharing plans are qualified plans where employers can make discretionary contributions that may vary from year to year. Each employee usually receives the same contribution percentage unless the plan is designed to take advantage of permitted disparity rules. Some of these permitted changes to contribution amounts for participants can be based on age or integrated with social security. It is also possible to assign classes to employees. These permitted disparity rules allow you to allocate a higher percentage of the dollars to the older or more highly compensated people in the practice. This will typically be the partners and associates. The contributions are usually based on business profits, but according to the IRS rules, you can also contribute to your plan based on compensation.

The maximum deductible contribution that can be made to a profit-sharing plan is 25 percent of "eligible" compensation to a maximum of $44,000 in 2006. Eligible compensation is all the compensation an employer pays to eligible plan participants during the employer's tax year. Contributions are tax-deductible, and earnings accumulate on a tax-deferred basis. The employer takes the deduction for this contribution. The employer's contribution to each employee's account is not considered taxable income to the employees for the contribution year. In very profitable practices or specialty clinics, it is common to see a profit-sharing plan together with a safe harbor 401k. Together, the limit is **still** $44,000. This way, the owners can contribute the $15,000 throughout the year and determine at the end of the year if they want to contribute the remaining $29,000.

SEP IRAs: An SEP IRA is very similar to a basic profit-sharing plan. The contribution limits are essentially the same. However, you are not allowed to put a vesting schedule on an SEP IRA. Once a contribution is made for an employee, the employer may not recoup any of the contribution if the employee terminates employment. You must include all employees that have worked in three of the last five years. You are permitted to allow sooner access to the plan, but not more restrictive.

401(k) plans: A 401(k) plan allows employees to defer their own money into the plan. In 2006, you can defer up to $15,000 into a 401(k). The employer may offer matching contributions and may impose a vesting schedule with respect to the employers matching funds. If you had a 401(k) with a 3 percent match, assuming $160,000 income, the total funding could be $19,800 ($15,000 + [$160,000 x 3 percent]). Having a vesting schedule means matched contributions would not be available to employees if they left the practice within a certain time period. A normal vesting schedule is 20 percent each year for five years. 401(k) plans do require more monitoring than SIMPLE IRAs. It is important to make sure your employees are contributing enough to a basic 401(k) plan or your plan may be deemed top-heavy, which limits your contribution amount.

ROTH 401(k) Option: As mentioned earlier, in 2006, the tax laws changed to allow 401(k) plans to receive "Roth 401(k)" deferrals. The advantage is if your income is too high for a regular ROTH, now you can qualify to make ROTH 401(k) contributions (up to $15,000 in 2006) through your firms 401(k) since there is no income qualification requirement. ROTH 401(k) deferrals however cost you the current income tax deduction you would have received if you were making regular pre-tax 401(k) deferrals. Also, you still will want to defer pre-tax the amount necessary to receive the maximum percentage your firm matches (do not miss the "free money"). You should consider making ROTH 401(k) deferrals only on the dollars you can defer above receiving the match. Keep in mind too, your firm has to amend its 401(k) plan document to allow ROTH 401(k) deferrals and if not, you are prevented from doing them.

"Safe harbor" 401(k) plans: A safe harbor 401(k) cannot be deemed top-heavy. It functions like a traditional 401(k) except the practice is required to make a contribution of 3 percent of compensation for everyone eligible. This is not a match. It is a required contribution and is vested immediately. If the employer is willing to contribute 3 percent of eligible payroll, the top-heavy testing is not necessary and the highly compensated owner can contribute the maximum amount each year.

Tax-sheltered annuity (TSA)/403(b) plans: If you work at a nonprofit organization, government agency or university, you can be offered the ability to defer into a TSA or 403(b). Most are not matched and are funded by your salary deferrals only. The deferral limits are now the same as those for 401(k)s, $15,000 annually for 2006.

If you own a practice and have not reviewed your qualified plan in the last three years, it would be advisable to look at your options. There have been many changes to qualified plans, with recent legislation making these plans much more attractive. It is important to have a clear vision of what you want the plan to accomplish before reviewing things. The main two issues to keep in mind would be:

- Do you want the plan to maximize your contribution with the lowest required contribution for your staff?

- Do you want to fund the plan so it is a retirement plan for you and your employees? In this case, you want the plan to be viewed a significant benefit of working for you and contributions to the plan should benefit both you and your employees.

Cash balance plans: If you have an interest, and your cash flow allows setting aside more than $44,000 per year pre-tax, there are additional options like cash balance plans. These plans normally make sense only for very productive practices with owners over the age of forty-five and a small number of young employees. If you are getting a late start in your planning, the plans can be worthwhile to consider.

In summary, qualified retirement plans are an integral part of your retirement, and there are many ways in which you can design a plan. It is important to make sure your advisor fully understands all the plan design options to create a plan that maximizes the benefits you want and minimizes negatives.

How Do I Best Plan for Retirement?

This is one of the common questions we get from most lawyers. Estimating your retirement needs is an important factor to consider in the Growth Accumulation Level of your plan. A financial planning rule of thumb is to figure on needing 80 percent of your pre-retirement take-home income, although more and more lawyers want a retirement lifestyle that is close to their working years (100 percent of pre-retirement income). This figure should be based on the income you plan to be earning at retirement age, not that which you are making today.

To estimate this, look at your current expenses; subtract the expenses and savings that will not be needed at retirement, and then add in extra expenses (travel, medical, long-term care, prescription medicines, etc.) that may be incurred during retirement. Consider the following:

- Will you still be paying a mortgage?
- Will you still have children in college?
- Do you anticipate hefty medical expenses for yourself or a spouse?
- Do you wish to travel extensively?
- Will your day-to-day living expenses be similar to or less than what they are now?

It is important to understand how your life will change during retirement and establish an overall retirement strategy that will allow you to enjoy retirement and provide you with the flexibility to deal with changes.

The underlying question to address in retirement is, "Will I ever run out of money?" Or, put another way, "How long will my money last?" People are living longer than ever, retirement is costing more than most people ever thought, and the government and law firm pension plans and retirement buyouts are providing less. As we said earlier, your financial house may need to be built much larger than you realize or you won't ever be able to completely retire. Historically, too many lawyers have had to work well beyond age sixty-five because they simply could not afford to retire. You cannot "borrow" money to solve the issue of not having enough retirement assets. The bottom line is that you do not want your money to run out before you do!

There are four main things you can do to avoid outliving your money:

1. **Save and invest** enough money from your current income as soon as possible.
2. **Earn a high enough rate of return** on your savings and investments.
3. **Delay Retirement.**
4. **Live on less** during retirement.

You need to be focused on the first two strategies above so you can avoid being forced to implement the less desirable third and fourth options. That is why we spend so much time with younger lawyers advising and coaching them about their cash flow, saving, and investing habits. The lawyers who implement positive saving and investing habits early in their law career will be the ones who are able to dictate when they retire and how comfortably. If you have not been able to implement the strategies we have shown you in this book, maybe it is time to hire a qualified financial advisor who understands the challenges you face as a lawyer to get you to do it. You make a good living, and you can pay someone to help you protect and help your assets to grow. Many top athletes do this by hiring professional trainers to help them achieve the peak level of performance they seek.

Another reason you want to get going as soon as possible with your financial house plan is to avoid the risk of being dependent on *having to* earn a specific rate of return. In other words, your small amount of retirement assets will run out long before you do unless you earn a really high rate of return over time. We call this being "return dependent" which—like co-dependent can mean an unhealthy reliance on someone else—your assets should not rely solely on the rate of return they earn to make them last throughout retirement. You have to also add to those assets—save and invest enough money regularly over a long enough time—to take the pressure off of those dollars *having to* earn huge returns each and every year, which is highly improbable. Do not be tempted to stop adding to your retirement investments, as there is not an investment we know of that provides a high enough return every year over a long period of time that can bail you out.

We also regularly caution our lawyer clients not to rely too heavily on benefits provided by their firms, especially those an individual can provide or at least supplement. This is not only because lawyers frequently change firms and thus benefit programs, but also because many have under-funded retirement plans. Firms are cutting back on benefits too; not adding to their profit-sharing plans as in the past because of budget concerns, firm mergers, and dissolutions. Also, previous promises of large firm buyouts at retirement frequently do not materialize as hoped. Realize that just because you are putting the maximum amount allowed into the firm's retirement plan, this alone may not be enough for you to retire on. The match on the

401(k) is a nice benefit, but it may not add up to be nearly enough if compared to what you need at retirement. When you are suddenly faced with scaled-down benefits that do not meet your lofty expectations, you can only wish you planned differently if you knew how unreliable those benefit plans would turn out to be.

Finally, do not withdrawal or loans from your retirement plan for current spending needs. So many lawyers cash in their 401(k) retirement plan accounts when they change jobs to pay off debts or buy cars and houses. This is a major impediment to building wealth, but it is one that can be easily avoided. We consider it a partial self-inflicted demolition of your own financial house. You are to be a financial home builder, not a financial home wrecker. It might solve your temporary debt issue, but it won't solve the bigger problems of not learning how to save better and spend less. Withdrawals from qualified plans before age fifty-nine and a half are subject to income taxes and penalties. In addition, the lost future growth on those taxes and penalties paid on the amount withdrawn as well makes this a very expensive way to "raise cash".

8

The Speculation Level

The speculation level involves risking money you can afford to lose. Imagine this level as the roof or last level of your financial house. Some people are never comfortable with speculative risks and thus should not consider it. These people should simply build their financial house wider. In fact, the more you maximize the strategies in building the other levels of your financial house (Chapters 4 through 6), the less you need to be aggressive and take speculative risks to achieve your long-term goals.

Subjecting your money where the principal has a high degree of volatility and risk has potentially high returns, but your money could also be lost completely. It is appropriate that speculating fits at the top of the financial house, because if the money is lost, it won't be devastating to your overall financial house plan.

A good rule of thumb when deciding how much to risk in a business opportunity or other aggressive venture is one year's worth of net worth growth. Never invest more than that! In a worst case scenario, if you lost the entire amount of your investment, you have basically lost one year's worth of financial progress. While not fun, it is not financially devastating. People get into trouble and can't recover financially when they take a lifetime worth of savings and gamble with it.

As an example, let's say your net worth is $200,000 and you project that a year from now, it will grow to $225,000. This growth could be from additional saving and investing, reducing debts, and/or growth from your existing assets. In any event, the $25,000 projected growth is the amount that could be considered for a very speculative investment.

In the event that an opportunity has come along which requires more than this amount, do not be tempted to risk more. Consider sticking to an area you know, lowering your investment, delaying the timing until your net worth has grown, or involving a financial partner.

This stage can involve different things for different people. It might mean going into solo practice or investing in very speculative individual stocks or aggressive specialty mutual funds. The following are just a few other examples of other speculative investments that exist:

- Buying raw land and/or highly leveraged real estate
- Buying stock in companies that have just gone public (via initial public offerings)
- Buying stocks with borrowed money (on margin or from a home equity loan)
- Investing in a friend's or family member's new small business
- Trading in commodities like gold, silver, and gemstones

Again, keep in mind that speculative investments, while valid financial tools, are typically used only by extremely savvy investors, high net worth investors, and institutions, and they are not recommended to anyone who cannot afford to lose a substantial amount of their net worth. These investments carry an extraordinary amount of risk, and they generally require intensive research and knowledge to carry out the investment.

In summary, no one has ever gotten into trouble financially by being too conservative for too long. Sure, there are some potential lost opportunity costs, but you can get into a lot of financial trouble by being too aggressive with too much money. That's why the financial house is such a useful tool to help organize and prioritize these decisions.

9

Summing Up

We started out identifying the many barriers you face as a lawyer that can prevent you from developing the wealth you desire. Throughout this book, we have made a case for the critical financial habits and strategies necessary for you to overcome those barriers. The blueprint for developing wealth is to build your financial house one level at a time from the bottom up.

Building a solid financial house of your dreams is a step-by-step process, not just picking and choosing areas to complete that seem more appealing. How can your house be structurally sound if you want to install the grand front entranceway when the cement blocks have not been set beneath it in the underlying foundation? Yet we see too many lawyers get ahead of themselves investing in risky areas before they secure properly designed insurance protection and have their cash flow under control. Building out of sequence often weakens the overall structure of your financial house, as money "leaks out" from investment assets that have to be sold prematurely to address emergencies that could have been better planned for. It is tempting to skip or ignore some of these areas, but we want to encourage you to build every strategy and feature into your financial house. They all work together to make it stand firm against the "bad weather" of unforeseen events that could tear it down.

As a young lawyer, you have the best chance of building the financial house of your dreams if you start applying these strategies **now**. You have the time to let money compound—the more you leave it invested, the more it has the potential to grow. You have the lifetime earning potential to reach your goals—if you plan ahead how to maximize its use and don't just always financially react. You also have the intelligence to put all the pieces together if you focus on an overall building plan and not just a few of the pieces.

What are you waiting for? Don't wait another day. Start applying what you have learned right in Chapter 1. You have to treat yourself as one of your most important clients. You spend so much of your day advocating for the needs of others, you need to give yourself permission to make yourself a priority as well. Having your finances in order will help you be a better lawyer. If you cannot get yourself to put all the pieces of your financial house in place, then it is time to hire a trusted financial advisor to help you build and maintain it. Your clients hire you as a legal professional, and you know the security they achieve through the work you do for them. The accountability provided by the right advisor can be just the catalyst you need to finally get your financial house in order.

We hope this book gives you the information you need to start building your financial house as quickly as possible or to repair the weaker parts of the financial structure you may have already started. As financial architects who advocate for the financial health of lawyers, we also hope to have encouraged you so that **you can** reach your dreams. Now we challenge you to make the time to build your financial house big enough to reach them.

ABOUT THE AUTHORS

Certified Financial Planner™ (CFP®) Practitioner Thomas A. Haunty has been practicing financial planning for individuals and businesses since 1982. He has further developed a practice subspecialty providing financial services for attorneys, their law firms, and their clients. Mr. Haunty has authored and been quoted in numerous articles on attorney finances published in *The ABA Journal.* He has also spoken nationally on helping lawyers maximize their finances at numerous bar association meetings, conventions, and law firms. In addition, he serves as the volunteer financial advisor for the American Bar Endowment (ABE), a not-for-profit arm of the American Bar Association, in its efforts to serve ABA Young Lawyers Division members.

Mr. Haunty has spent his career with the financial services firm of North Star Resource Group, one of the oldest and largest independent financial services firms in the country. He is a senior partner in the firm's Madison, Wisconsin, branch office and manages in excess of $116 million (as of December 30, 2005) for clients across the country.

In addition to receiving his undergraduate business degree as an Evans Scholar from the University of Wisconsin–Madison and his certified financial planner™ (CFP®) designation, Mr. Haunty is accredited as a registered health underwriter (RHU), a registered employee benefits consultant (REBC), and a chartered financial consultant (ChFC). Mr. Haunty is also an associate member of the American Bar Association, a member of the Financial Planning Association, a member of the Financial Counseling and Employee Benefits Sections of the Society of Financial Services Professionals™, and a life and qualifying member of the Million Dollar Round Table, the premier association of financial professionals®.

Certified Financial Planner™ (CFP®) Practitioner Todd D. Bramson has been working in the field of financial planning for more than twenty years. An exceptional teacher, motivating author, and speaker, he has been quoted in numerous financial publications and spent several years as the financial expert on the local NBC live 5:00 p.m. news broadcast. In June of 2004, he spoke at the prestigious Million Dollar Round Table, a worldwide organization of the top 5 percent of all financial services professionals. Mr.

Bramson's belief that "If the trust is there, the miles don't matter" has earned him devoted clients not only in his hometown of Madison, Wisconsin, but in almost every state in the country.

Along with all the advanced designations expected of a trusted financial professional, he is committed to keeping abreast of all the developments in his field and to playing an active role in his community. Mr. Bramson conducts regular public seminars and is active in his church, the Breakfast Optimist Club, Evans Scholars Alumni Foundation, and Blackhawk Country Club.

CFP® and Certified Financial Planner™ are certification marks owned by the Certified Financial Planner Board of Standards Inc. These marks are awarded to individuals who successfully complete the CFP Board's initial and ongoing certification requirements.

NORTH STAR RESOURCE GROUP

One of the oldest and largest independent
financial services firms in the United States**

Both Tom and Todd are senior partners
in the Madison, Wisconsin, branch office
of North Star Resource Group and
investment advisor representatives of

CRI Securities, LLC and Securian Financial Services, Inc.,
registered investment advisors.
CRI Securities, LLC is affiliated with
Securian Financial Services, Inc.

Thomas A. Haunty, CFP®, RHU, REBC, ChFC
E-mail: thomas.haunty@northstarfinancial.com
1-608-271-9100, ext. 216 or
1-888-655-8091, ext. 216
Web site: www.tomhaunty.com

Todd D. Bramson, CFP®, ChFC, CLU
E-mail: todd.bramson@northstarfinancial.com
1-608-271-9100, ext.218
Web site: www.toddbramson.com

North Star Resource Group
2945 Triverton Pike Drive, Suite 200
Madison, WI 53711

**Sources: GAMA International, North Star's
corporate origins trace back to 1908 in St. Paul, Minnesota

Tax Disclosure

The information in this book regarding relevant federal tax laws is only a general discussion and overview. It is not intended for nor can it be used for any taxpayer for the purpose of avoiding federal tax penalties. This information is intended to support the promotion or marketing of ideas that may benefit a taxpayer. Taxpayers should seek the advice of their own tax and legal advisors regarding any tax or legal issues applicable to their specific circumstances.

This book is not an offer to buy or a solicitation to sell any investment security. Variable life insurance, variable annuities, and mutual funds are sold only by a current prospectus. The prospectus contains important information you should carefully consider about the product's charges, expenses, risks, and other relevant information associated with the product. You should always read the prospectus carefully before investing.

This book contains a lot of information and investment/planning strategies. Since everyone's financial situation is different, the strategies and concepts discussed within this book may not be appropriate for everyone. You should consult with your own independent financial, legal, and/or tax advisor(s) before implementing any financial, legal, or tax strategy.

We do not practice law, accounting, and/or offer specific tax advice, and it is not our purpose to do so in this book.

The tax concepts that are addressed in this book are current as of 2006. Tax laws change frequently, and any tax concept addressed in this book may not be applicable after 2006.

Specific tax consequences addressing 529 College Savings Plans or dividend and capital gain taxation are all subject to a sunset provision. Unless these are signed into permanent law, the favorable tax provisions are subject to expire between January of 2008 and December 31, 2010.

Thomas A. Haunty and Todd D. Bramson are both investment advisor representatives with CRI Securities, LLC and Securian Financial Services, Inc., Registered investment advisors

Tracking #: 2006 716 MA1
DOFU: 07/06